Bipolar and Pregnant

Katie McDowell

Correspondence may be sent to AuthorKatieMcDowell@gmail.com.
Copyright © 2017 by Katie McDowell. All rights reserved.

From the Author:

I didn't think I'd write a memoir like this until I was old and grey, perhaps only then assuming any semblance of wisdom worthy of penning into a personal account. Instead, you get to meet me now, with all of my raw emotions through the chaos of my two new coinciding challenges of bipolar disorder and pregnancy. I am scared and brave, weak and strong, and throughout my journal, I hope you'll see that I am real.

My real name, however, is not Katie McDowell. All the names and places here are using pseudonyms, but the book is wholly true.

My pregnancy did not follow a textbook norm. If you've ever sat around with decaf lattes at your local coffeehouse with a handful of pregnant women, you'll know there's no such thing as a normal pregnancy. All sorts of things can, and often do, happen in pregnancy, like maternal illness, fetal development problems, rollercoaster emotions, and life itself. Yes, life itself continues onward through pregnancy, and this can be enriched by countless joys and fraught with infinite struggles.

The struggle of bipolar disorder entered my life the same time pregnancy did. Just as all pregnancies are different, there is no such thing as a prototypical bipolar patient. I have too many variables that influence my bipolar disorder to be your perfect little vignette. Plus, given that this book only follows my first nine months after diagnosis, both my disorder and I will continue changing. You'll see how my supportive husband, my comorbid PTSD, my spiritual faith, and all my big and little character traits shape who I am as a woman with bipolar disorder. We truly are all unique.

Though there are infinite variations of bipolar disorder, there are also important unifying elements, which help to know how to understand the illness and the best ways to treat it. Throughout my book, I have carefully included information and facts from reliable scientific publications to make this more than just a memoir of mine but also a gentle educational book. I knew very little about bipolar disorder when I was diagnosed, so the information threaded throughout my book is authentically enmeshed with my nine-month journey, where I read and learned and wrote through everything that happened.

Writing this book came very easy to me and was a joy to create. But it could not have been possible without the special individuals I'd like to thank:

For my husband "Eric". I know you love all of me. Thank you for your endless devotion to me, your thoughtfulness each day, and your encouraging spirit. You have never let go of my hand. Thank you for consistently striving to be the outstanding husband you are. Thank you for being you. I am amazed at how blessed I am to be married to you. I love all of you.

For "Holly", my kindhearted therapist. Thank you for tirelessly supporting me through soaring heights and through the darkest lows. Thank you for showing me how to find my own insight, which made this book possible, and which continues to guide me toward what I should do with my one wild and precious life.

For my psychiatrist "Dr. C". How ever were you the first person I told I was pregnant?! Because of your calm and caring spirit. Thank you for being my trustworthy physician. Good luck at your next race.

"Katie McDowell"
July, 2017

Chapter 1: Weeks 1-4

I am pregnant. And I have bipolar disorder.

Both of these diagnoses are brand new to me, and they both came within a week of each other. They were a shock, and each came as bad news—the bipolar disorder because, well, who wants to have bipolar disorder? And since I found out I was pregnant right after I found out I had bipolar disorder, I wondered, how could I manage becoming a mother and take on two life-changing challenges at once?

My name is Katie McDowell, and this is my journal on the nine months before Baby is born.

On a Monday night, oblivious I was three and a half weeks pregnant, I left Springview Hospital in a lovely suburb of the city, discharged with a not-so-lovely diagnosis: bipolar disorder.

Well, Springview isn't really the name of the hospital. And I'll let you in on another secret: My name really isn't Katie McDowell. In writing this true account of events, I am choosing to keep all personal names anonymous with pseudonyms. This is because: A) I respect others' privacy, B) Sometimes I and others behave…not so ideally, and C) Probably what I've been consumed the most about lately—I don't want to attach my real name to "bipolar disorder." I'm shocked that it really is, and I'll admit I'm still stung with shame and confusion.

About a month before my discharge from Springview, after a transcontinental red-eye flight back home during the Columbus Day weekend, I hopped on the train straight from the airport to the university where I worked as a research coordinator in genetics and nutrition. Always a light sleeper, I've never been able to sleep on planes. I had planned a much earlier arrival that would have allowed me a nice nap at home before work, but a significant flight delay ruined that plan, and I never caught any Zzz's.

Today, as I write this, I blame a certain airline a little bit for all that happened afterward. Blaming feels good. Right now, I feel like someone should be held responsible, and I really don't want it to be me. It's not my fault I developed bipolar disorder.

...Or is it? My heart is a bit sunken.

After my fun Columbus Day weekend trip, for the next three weeks, I progressively needed less and less sleep each night, until I could only nap 3-4 hours somewhere between 1-5am. Yet, rather miraculously, I felt excellent during the day and never missed the sleep. No yawns, no groggy thoughts. And no concerns, either.

Before I go on, I need to tell you a little about my Usual Self. I have always been an outgoing introvert. By that I mean I have no trouble making friends and am not shy, but I need plenty of Katie Time. Most people probably think of me as an extrovert, but they don't know that I recharge while alone. I enjoy routine alone activities—reading, writing, running. Too much time around people and I always manage to sneak away for a breather. My hugest concern about getting married—which I did over a year ago—was I'd suffocate to death under the constant presence of a husband. Marriage fortunately turned out to give me plenty of the space I crave, but let's just say my worries about it gave me cold feet more than once.

That's another aspect about me—I'm a worrier. I wouldn't say I worry frenetically, but give me an ounce of negative information

Bipolar and Pregnant

and I'll worry it'll morph into a pound if I don't squash it with some good worrying. I'm pretty good at letting go of worries before they paralyze me to death. Usually. But I'll admit, lately I've been drugging myself with over-the-counter sleep aids at night to dampen out my anxiety enough to sleep.

One last aspect to describe about myself for now is that I'm very disciplined and love routine. I was a world-ranked swimmer in college and even as a young child built in habits of discipline that I now feel most at home with. I exercise regularly, I get ample sleep, and I eat a balanced diet. I'm careful with money and try to be careful with my words. I monitor and limit my own screen time. My home is always clean, and I don't procrastinate. I read a whole lot, and I always make sure I include nonfiction educational material, because I believe learning should be lifelong. I am a planner. I am not impulsive or adventurous, and I love the comfort of a good comfort zone.

So when I started revving up with energy and needing much less sleep, my Usual Self would have been bothered by this, would have consulted a physician or at least WebMD, and would have set up plenty of safeguards around me to be sure my own behaviors and health were not in jeopardy.

But, as I've now learned is almost universally common for first experiences with the mania of bipolar disorder, I became the happy-go-lucky person I've always wished to become and experienced all the warning signs that Something Is Amiss without an inkling of a worry.

A date I need to mention here is October 14—the Friday after Columbus Day, when I was feeling excellent. As an OB calculates it, your first week of pregnancy, as it's charted during its approximately 40-week course, begins on the date of your last period. This is where the story technically begins.

Katie McDowell

Hypomanic, I was a well-oiled machine. In fact, I've never functioned better. Work was a breeze, and my social life was soaring. I began double and even triple-layering my evenings with various outings and dinners with girlfriends. My husband Eric didn't seem to mind. After work, I'd work out, then go to a class or meet a friend at a restaurant, and then catch up with another friend over a drink. I craved sex (and Eric definitely didn't seem to mind). Life was glorious.

I mean this quite literally—life was glorious. Food tasted exquisite, and I wanted to try everything. I sought out the best wines. My spiritual life was rich; I sensed God's presence. The autumn trees were absolutely magnificent—everything was beautiful! I tried photographing everything, but the world was just too fast to capture. The breeze at night was a celestial wind stringing magic through the old streets of the city and swirling its wisps of otherworldliness through my soul. I felt amazing.

I *was* amazing. Late at night, when I couldn't sleep and didn't want to anyway, I talked excitedly with my husband of all my great ideas. I had many poetic visions and about eleven novels to write, overlapping and blending together in my increasingly speedy mind. I was on fire.

My friends didn't seem to notice any changes. Maybe I hadn't yet shifted enough on the outside for there to have been anything to notice. I barely noticed, myself.

I was exuberant, but I told myself, and later my husband and my therapist and my psychiatrist, I was simply being My Best Me, and this was certainly not a cause for concern but celebration!

However, my Usual Self was still there, too, deep down. It had been watching me with admiration, of my ambition and charisma. The Usual Self who is realistic and only mildly and rarely dabbles in optimism was a little suspicious of my newfound overflowing confidence and surety. My Usual Self who runs a very tight ship and is not spontaneous, sleeps a rather precise eight point five hours every night, and prefers the safety of limitations recognized something was off.

But everything I was enjoying lulled my Usual Self to the background and told her she needed a vacation. My exuberant joy yelled to the sky that it was all right, and brilliantly so.

I felt Perfect.

Despite the nightly productivity, I aimed to take care of myself and two weeks into these heights felt I might eventually succumb to fatigue and need to compensate for the insomnia (which actually isn't technically insomnia if the sleeplessness doesn't make you tired). I tried going to bed earlier and leaving the Kindle untouched. I tried ever-increasing doses of Benadryl. I simply couldn't sleep, and even with all my knowledge about the biochemical importance of sleep for my mind and body, I felt too damn good to worry.

And then I saw Holly.

Holly is my therapist. At this point in my life, having known Holly over a year and having been miraculously kept afloat with Holly's help during two episodes of depression in that time—one so severe it required an entire month's hospitalization at Springview, I was ready to say farewell to her. Obviously, a therapist appointment was a complete waste of time when there were so many other important—rather *urgent*—breathtaking things to do in the world while hypomanic.

Holly used the "B" word first, and as I recall she seemed more cautious than hesitant. She knew me well enough to know that I would, as I indeed did, dismiss her with a little laugh. Hypomania, oh brother! I wasn't having any problems with mental health. My mental health had never been *health*ier. I was my Best Self! I felt Perfect! I definitely did not believe this luxurious energy and creativity needed, preposterously, treatment!

Holly explained how my hyperactivity—and notice my talkativeness?—and insomnia were rather hallmark symptoms of hypomania of Bipolar II disorder. She jogged my memory to the two short periods of five to seven days I'd had two and three years prior of a similar but more muted exuberance. She reminded me about my three family members with bipolar disorder and my genetic susceptibility. And she explained that poor insight while feeling perfect might cloud my judgment and ability to recognize escalations and problems—escalations that could result in a crash from great heights down into depression.

The "D" word scares the living shite out of me. At this point in my journal, I need to pause and back up a little to give you a brief personal mental health history. There needs to be some background so that you can maybe understand how this bipolar diagnosis came about.

I'll leave it to you to figure out what caused the pregnancy diagnosis.

I have had five bad episodes of depression—two of which required hospitalizations. My first depression followed right after a traumatic event in my life: I was raped by a friend. I didn't tell anyone, and the PTSD was devastating. I began having panic attacks and was pretty sure I had the symptoms of depression. (Um, duh—but give me some slack—I was a total newbie to Mental Health Problems.) I found a psychiatrist, started antidepressants and benzos, and felt a bit better.

And so I quit them, of course.

Bipolar and Pregnant

Within weeks, I was worse than before. My dissociation had taken on a life of its own, and I thought about suicide all the time. I kept this up a long while, until I could no longer. I tried to kill myself, with a whole bottle of Tylenol. Twice. After that, I was dragged to help. I started seeing a therapist regularly, and I truly began to heal.

After I'd enjoyed a good period of stability, I took a break from therapy. I also dropped medications. Things were going mostly great—until, five years after being raped, I wanted to start dating again. PTSD reared its ugly head, and I was ready to kick it in the balls. So I found Lindsay.

Lindsay is a clinical psychologist and a prolific PTSD researcher. I trusted her as an expert, and later as a warm ally. As a trauma survivor, a child of divorced parents, and an adult with perpetual "Middle Child Syndrome", I benefited a lot from therapy with Lindsay. Lindsay also encouraged me to return to taking an anti-depressant as a sensible, proven prevention plan, so I did with my primary care physician. I connected well with her, and she helped me develop my own insight and problem-solving abilities. Doubtless, without Lindsay, I'd have never allowed myself to be vulnerable enough to even consider marrying Eric. I was very open with Lindsay—more open than I'd ever been with anyone in my life.

So, naturally I told her about my Hyper Week. My five to seven days during grad school when I was quite—as I simply put it—"hyper." It was a wonderful week, I'd told Lindsay. I had lots of really great ideas, and I was sleeping maybe a bit less, but—no worries!—I wasn't tired.

I told Lindsay about the project that had found its way into my speeding mind that week—how I'd planned to map out the molecular connections between a whole variety of chronic diseases. Fair enough, at first glance. I had been taking a graduate course in biochemistry and disease, and I'd been inspired with their interconnections. But I'd only been learning about the tip-top surface of molecular pathways of disease; yet I was certain I'd develop the first Great Map for them all. To begin, I went to the store, bought four white posters, and went home and taped them together, to start penciling my map.

I'm quite sure I minimized the project with Lindsay, and I'm certain I didn't tell her what was most important at the time to me: the urgency that I complete it *that night*.

It was bizarre for me especially, because, as I've said, I'm a planner. I'm methodical. I hesitate at Grand Ideas. I like to chew things over and consider if they're practical and realistic. But the next morning, in seeing my makeshift whiteboard on the kitchen table, hardly drawn upon—I'd gotten distracted, apparently—I simply had a little chuckle to myself and happily let it go. I *knew* I had acted outside of my Usual Self, but I felt so good all over that it didn't feel appropriate to scold myself for doing something silly.

After a few days, I simply noticed during the day that I wasn't quick anymore, and I didn't have extra energy. The Hyper Week had passed.

"Have you ever noticed anything like this before?" Lindsay asked me when I next saw her, in her office near a beautiful body of water.

"No," I answered. It was all a bit funny, really. And then my mind snagged a memory up like a silk blouse in a trousers zipper.

"Well," I thought, recalling. "There was a similar week last year…"

Bipolar and Pregnant

I told her about the week I volunteered at an art camp for homeless kids in the city, during a week off in a wonderful internship at a hospital. I led art groups for the older kids, focusing on emotional expression through an array of media—dance, painting, clay sculpting, music, and writing. I'd been unusually hyper that week too, and, yes, my thoughts did seem to be rushing, I remembered. But, again, it simply died down.

Lindsay and I kept talking, and she wanted me to keep an eye out for these feelings of hyperactivity and any changes in my sleep pattern. As I drove home from my appointment, I found myself nostalgic for that week. I was feeling so *connected* with everyone. The whole world made perfect sense, and I was *integral* to it too.

The following year, seemingly out of nowhere, Depression #3, or D3, I'll call it, hit. I remembered perfectly well what depression had felt like, four years before. But it wasn't quite the same. It didn't come on with an identifiable trigger, and it wasn't intertwined with all the flashbacks, panic, and dissociation as before. It slithered up on me like a wicked boa and was wrapped around me before I even noticed I was about to be fatally constricted.

That year was my clinical internship year. I simply couldn't afford a depression. I looked up the psychiatrist, Dr. J, who had been the Resident seeing me during D2 when I was a colossal mess, and she warmly welcomed me to see her in her private practice. With Dr. J, Lindsay, and the long-distance support of my fiancée Eric, I scratched and clawed my way through those dark nights of the soul, and it was over in less than three months. I kicked butt in the internship, went off to Hawaii to marry Eric, and then moved into this fun new city where I now live.

After three episodes of excruciating depression, I was proactive in its prevention. The first week in the city, I met with two different therapists and chose the one I clicked best with—Holly.

Whereas Lindsay, who I had to leave behind when I moved, was encouraging in a coach-like way and was very matter-of-fact, Holly is warmth and reflection. Lindsay was stilettos and makeup; Holly is naturally perfect in neutrals of comfort. Accurate or not, I would imagine my most exciting Friday nights are Lindsay's everyday nights, and my ideal Saturday mornings—on a porch swing with a hot coffee and a book—are Holly's ideal everyday mornings. They're very different. Yet, they've each been awesome at what they do, for me and with me in therapy, in their own ways.

Holly connected me with a psychiatrist, who we'll just call Dr. C. Dr. C is maybe a decade older than me (I'm 32), and I suspect we have a little bit in common. I'm a poet who reads all the latest research in nutrition science. On the wall in his office, he has a metal chemical structure of serotonin; on the next wall is a beautiful van Gogh. I'll bet he's super smart, but I could find loads of smart doctors in this city. I like Dr. C because he's careful, humble, and, in an easy-going quirky way, relatable with me.

Within weeks of moving to this new city to be with Eric, D4 hit. Similar to D3, I clawed through it, with all its blackness, endless fatigue, and suicidal thoughts. It ended within 3-4 months too, but this time, afterward I felt really baffled—and let down.

I was doing all the Right Things. I had been taking the stupid anti-depressant, going to weekly therapy sessions, and really working on my thinking patterns and behaviors in my new marriage. Depression seemed to be completely outside myself and take over me like a phantom. Depression seemed to be completely indifferent to all my hard efforts. Was I wasting my time and energy?

And then Daniel died. Or, to be accurate, Daniel killed himself.

Dan was a friend from home. I had befriended his wife Jane at church, and I sat next to them on the pew each Sunday. Several times, I visited Jane and Dan at their home, and they took care of me as though I were their daughter. I love Jane. And I loved Dan.

Dan had bipolar disorder.

When I got off the phone with Jane one evening, after crying with her, my sweet friend, I thought about all the dark suicidal thoughts I'd had in the Depression #4 that had just lifted—and all the depressions preceding it. I didn't want to leave Eric like Daniel left Jane. I wanted to live life.

My first two suicidal depressions, I hadn't been on an antidepressant, and I felt that a few weeks after I started taking it, the depression started to improve. But the past two depressions, I'd already been taking the SSRI antidepressant when they hit, so I felt like I didn't have as much ammo left to shoot at the depression. Therefore, like a fully educated and trained psychiatrist, I decided it would be better to stop taking the SSRI and hold it for an onset of depression symptoms.

The next month, I saw Dr. C my psychiatrist and told him I'd quit my medication.

After a reflexive twitch to that, he calmly said, "You what?"

I knew it sounded risky, non-compliant, Taking Matters Into My Own Stupid Hands. But to me it had seemed very reasonable and the best safeguard to fight depression if it hit again. And, at this point, I had stopped saying "If" and traded it for "When". I believed the phantom would be back, and I couldn't bear to look into the eyes of that Monster of Horror again without some assurance that I had a weapon reserved for it.

What I thought back then was, I didn't really trust Dr. C. How much could he really know me? He was probably taking the average, the generalized, the impersonal route with me, following some pharmacological algorithm cross-checked and verified with a series of ICD codes and manuals.

But, really, I didn't trust myself. I didn't trust I could follow through with Living and fight my way through ever again. Even if it was a placebo effect, and I played some twisted mind games with myself knowing I was purposefully setting myself up for a potential placebo effect, I wanted to have some Hope on reserve. In case I became Hopeless, like Daniel.

As I told you, I was an elite swimmer in my youth and in college. If anyone knows about the importance of the—to me, Sacred—mutual trust between Coach and Athlete, I do. My coach entrusted the work ethic and unrelenting determination necessary to take me to the next level of competition to me; I entrusted the overarching plan of how to get there to my coach. I had excellent relationships with them. I loved working with them, and I know with a sparkle in their eyes, they loved working with me too.

Now, I could write a book on the ways my trust in other people—people who were supposed to uphold my safety and my wellbeing—has been let down. Shattered, more like. Maybe most people could write that book too. But since the storm of betrayals (including rape) several years ago, I've done loads of therapy. I've turned over some major frickin leaves. So I know this partnership I need with Dr. C won't work if I don't at least trust him a little and have faith that with him and Holly, I can get through Come What May if I really want to.

D5 came only three months later.

This was this past summer, and I conceived Baby in late October, so I need to move it along and catch you up to the present.

Besides, I don't feel like talking about D5 right now. I just don't have it in me to think about it. I'll just say it took a month at Springview Hospital before I was out of the pitch-black darkness.

After D5, I was resolved to stay on meds again. I promised my inpatient doctor Dr. Douglas I would stick with Dr. C's plan. And I did.

I also kept up with therapy. At Holly's encouragement, I also started seeing Meg, a trauma therapist, who could help me with some lingering PTSD problems I was having. Between the three of my Support Team, I was seeing a mental health provider at least every week.

Mania is deceiving. It's intoxicating; your senses and thinking are not fully accurate. So when it creeps up, especially if it has never before been a problem and you don't know what warning signs to be aware of, it is very easy to brush off.

When the sleeplessness began, I dismissed it. When my mood began soaring, I enjoyed it. When my mind began rushing, mostly with Great Ideas, I celebrated them.

When Holly showed concern, it seemed all out of place. Concern was meant for struggles to get out of bed, for suicidal thoughts, for the brutal torture called Day and Godless horror called Night during depression. This didn't make sense.

Holly said, "Will you please schedule an appointment with Dr. C? And is it OK if I talk with him?"

I agreed, because I whole-heartedly believed Dr. C would see that I was perfectly fine. A little hyperactivity never hurt anyone, right? It would all blow over.

But, a couple days later, Dr. C agreed with Holly.

In this brief period of time, I had noticed something... *Not Perfect* about how I was feeling. An irritability had popped up, here and there. I snipped at Eric a few times with a feistiness unlike my Usual Self.

Dr. C said he believed I was hypomanic, like Holly had said. Hypomania is similar to mania, and indeed is the stage before a full-blown mania, where losing touch with reality and dangerous recklessness can occur. Hypomania is the highest high of Bipolar II, a form of bipolar disorder where depressions can be very severe, the manic phases less so.

Dr. C wanted me to start taking lithium. And, as I'd told him at my last appointment a couple weeks prior that Eric and I were going to stop using contraception and see if we'd get pregnant, he told me I should use contraception again for now. He also told me how to taper off my anti-depressant—the anti-depressant it had taken me several years to finally accept.

I was a bit dumbfounded by all this. But I said I would take the medicine. I reasoned to myself, "Who cares about taking lithium. I'm sure it couldn't hurt!" And then I let my blissful mood carry myself to the drugstore where I filled my first ever bottle of a mood stabilizer.

Bipolar and Pregnant

That night, however, as I pulled out a pill to swallow, I couldn't. Was I really about to take lithium? I also thought of the two weeks of unprotected sex Eric and I had, and I worried about the very small possibility I could have conceived and didn't know if that would change the medical approach to my symptoms.

So I didn't take the pill. I emailed Dr. C the next day, told him I was uncomfortable with the diagnosis and medicine, and he responded very kindly, expressing he understood my concerns and asked me to visit his office again to talk them through.

But—and this all happened so quickly—before that appointment, the hypomania was quickly turning sour. I felt extremely restless and irritable. I felt like I was Crawling in My Skin. I didn't know what to do.

A confounding factor in this is I very recently found out I have Graves' disease—an autoimmune hyperthyroid condition, which can cause weight loss (it did) despite increased appetite (I was eating like a linebacker basically), insomnia (huh!), anxiety, and, lo-and-behold, irritability. So maybe all these changes were simply due to too much thyroid hormone.

Only a few days before, I was feeling so Perfect I was ready to say farewell to Holly. Now, I was desperate for relief.

Rather than wait around for blood test results, Dr. C and I decided I'd go to the ER. They gave me a mild sedative prescription, told me my thyroid hormones were now actually in normal range, told me my urine pregnancy test was negative, and I went home.

But my mind rushed onward, and I became increasingly irritable. It progressed as the day went on. I started out the day—in a great mood, definitely—with about an average pace of thoughts. Whereas usually it takes me a big cup of coffee and a loop around the park walking the dogs to wake up to full sentences of thinking, I woke up Sharp and Ready to Go. My thoughts sped up, and came rushing quicker and quicker, and by the end of the day, they were rushing past one another, all vying for preeminence in my brain, like half a dozen horses at the Kentucky Derby necking it out, pulling ahead and falling behind, one after the other, all the way to the finish line.

Dr. C checked in with me via email, and I emailed back something along the lines of (I deleted this thread—you'll see why), "Well my mood is grand, my body feels like crap, and the agitation is so bad I wish I were dead."

I went to work. The day flew by. I had thought I liked my job all right in research, but much of the time the work was mundane. So when your mind is bubbling over with eagerness to pursue Great Ideas, your mostly administrative job can feel like a mostly Waste of Time. I thought of that numerous times these days— how I was better suited for Something Else, but what with my thoughts rushing at 90mph, I didn't ever think about it for very long. The afternoon and time to leave came up each day quickly, and I happily shut down my computer, locked my office door, and grabbed my bright neon running shoes to hit the trails.

That night I ran one of my favorite nine mile loops from the office down a historic landscaped path, around a big pond that always reflects light with a glow, and back.

I could have run it twice.

I came home to Eric, we had sex in the shower (get over it, prudes), I made something very rich and loaded with butter for dinner, followed by something very rich and loaded with sugar for dessert, and we got in bed.

Bipolar and Pregnant

Eric falls asleep fast. He twitches when his muscles relax as he dozes off, so when the stillness follows, I know he's out. Over nine times out of ten, Eric falls asleep before me.

I sighed. I was bored and Totally Not Sleepy.

I whipped out my phone and checked my emails, noting one from Dr. C.

"Dear Katie," it began, then with something like, "I'm sorry you're not feeling well, but please don't reference suicidal thoughts over email. If these are occurring you need to call me; these are not appropriate over email." I'm not sure what followed or if I even read it.

Revved in half a second, I let out a fiercely irritated little grunt. Eric stirred at that, so I slipped out of bed and went to my desk in the guest room, where I could type out an "appropriate" email in reply. Satisfied, I then proceeded to dust all the furniture, fold a load of laundry, read a chapter in a philosophy book, take more Benadryl, and go back to bed.

The next morning, I got up before Eric and made him waffles, brought them to bed with coffee on a platter. I sent him off to work with a kiss.

And then I saw my open laptop.

I never understood my girlfriends in college who, after a night out with a couple delicious cosmopolitans or Diet Cokes with Malibu, found it absolutely essential to whip out their tiny Nokia phones from their butt-hugging back pockets and text away at either their ex-boyfriend telling them off, again, or their current boyfriends for not like returning their texts like all day.

Katie McDowell

I read my email to Dr. C, and I swear I understood exactly how those girls must have felt the morning after.

I apparently had felt it very necessary to tell Dr. C that, thanks for his concern, but I no longer needed his help *ever* again, thankyouverymuch. And then I proceeded to spell out "Fourteen Examples of How Wanting to Die Can Be Used Colloquially", and how obviously he was a melodramatic freak to think I was serious.

It might not have been that harsh. It probably wasn't. I hope it wasn't. Honestly, I'm a nice girl. I don't ruffle feathers. I hate confrontation. Eric and I are both Stuffers, and actually engaging in conflict—and trust me, ours is wimpy—has been a big problem I've been working on with Holly. I've never blasted out an email like that before. It was like I was drunk.

But I wasn't. I was mentally ill.

During office hours, at work at the university, I slipped into the building's breast pumping room, locked the door, and left Dr. C a voice message, pretty desperately apologizing for the outrageous barrage.

He called back soon after. When I began to apologize again, he cut me off.

"Katie, I know you're not yourself, and I've already erased it from memory. Please don't apologize. Forgotten. But we need to come up with a plan, and I want to include Holly on this too."

I told him I liked the sound of a plan and that I was crawling in my skin with agitation again. Then, wounded, I confided in him: I was scared.

Bipolar and Pregnant

That night I was admitted to Springview Hospital. Less than four months after my discharge from the exact same unit.

This time, however, was very different. For one, as the mania picked up during the day and I was feeling fabulous again—almost convincing me to call off all plans and forget about treatment, I wasn't bothered about going in for admission. Knowing all the rules of the unit, I knew how to pack, remembering all the essentials you'd want to get you through a few days and nights, and remembering what all to leave behind.

Eric drove me the quick trip there. I turned up the radio, rolled down the window, and sang along to Adele, Sia, Ariana, and even (it was mental illness, I swear) Bieber from my car's speakers.

Also, this time, instead of being mute and hunched over in the intake room with the admissions psychiatrist, I found myself going through the story like I was unfolding an exciting movie plot, highlighting the interesting parts, and loving using my wit to make the fellow laugh, too.

That night, I started a beginner's dose of lithium and a sedating atypical antipsychotic. They also gave me some Ativan to help me chill down, and told me to come back for more of the latter two if I couldn't sleep.

By 1:30am, I was back at the med window.

It didn't take long at all, though, to notice a significant reduction in my agitation and rushing mind. In fact, on the 3rd night there, I slept through the night.

The six-day hospitalization went by quickly. I read, did cardio on a yoga mat in one of the big group rooms, and went to a few groups. I wished I had access to a punching bag and a jumprope, to hopefully burn away some of the energy that felt like was eventually going to explode. Unlike the summer, where it took everything in me to say just one thing and participate in a group—this time I had to keep apologizing for myself and shut the heck up. I felt really guilty amongst a group of mostly severely depressed people for feeling so, well, happy.

I wasn't so happy at work on Tuesday, the day after I was discharged. The department administrative director called me into her office, told me I'd missed too many days, and asked me to resign.

JOLT!

I was a hard worker. I was conscientious, quite perfectionistic, and a cheerful team player. My previous employers loved me. This wasn't the sort of thing that happened to me.

Bipolar disorder wasn't the sort of thing that happened to me either, though.

I responded well and agreed to think things over. Inside, I was so ashamed...and crushed.

Around 2008, a couple of my friends who like me were recent college grads, lost their jobs. I took for granted that my industry was rather recession-proof. I felt horrible for them. But—probably because nothing like that had ever come close to happening to me before—I have to admit, I do remember thinking, "It's a good thing I've made myself *indispensible* at my job. In doing the work of, like, two people, nobody would ever let *me* go." I couldn't imagine the blow to the self-esteem losing a job would take.

Please forgive the egotism. I've grown a lot since then. When your family cracks apart the same time as you're raped by a friend the same time as you experience your first horrible depression, you eventually learn that you actually can't control everything.

And now, basically what happened to my friends years ago was happening to me. Talk about kicked when you're down.

But…only a few weeks ago, I called in sick, in the hospital for two days for an attack of the GI disease called Crohn's that I have. Before Springview, that day in the ER was a workday. Six days at Springview—four of those were workdays. And, as this director brought up, I missed a whole month over the summer. Each times, I had the hospital staff send the appropriate note to my HR department, so at least I had been keeping up with proper documentation. But those were a lot of absences.

"It simply isn't working out," she said.

Eric was helpful. He reminded me of my many excited talks about other ideas I had during hypomania and how I'd been quite sure I wanted to quit my job anyway. He also brought up disability and employment laws, and assured me if I wanted to stay, I could. I'd had weekly meetings with the principal investigators I worked under, and I'd never received a single complaint. It truly was a stunner.

But at the same time, I understood. I wasn't reliable. Though I couldn't help it, they couldn't help it either.

Worse, I didn't believe I *could* be reliable. With all that had happened the past 6 months, I simply didn't feel any confidence that I could dig my heels into the ground and proclaim, "Things Will Be Different."

I met with my HR contact that week. She echoed my director: They were sorry but it wasn't working out. I wasn't a good fit for the role. And, she asked contemplatively, was the role really a good fit for me?

I thought about that. I hadn't minded my job before the hypomanic episode. It wasn't a dream job, but it was all right. With all my Great Ideas, maybe I'd been onto something for real—maybe it *was* time to leave.

I wished I had screwed up on the job. I wished I made a huge mistake or I'd gotten sloppy, or *something* that I could have *changed*. I felt helpless over this new sucky diagnosis and helpless over not being a rock star at my job.

I had a lot of competing thoughts for What To Do, but, thankfully, Eric and I had a 3-day weekend for Veteran's Day. I'd let this problem simmer and come back to it later.

We took an overnight trip to a great little town two hours away, and my spirits lifted. Over old-fashioned ice cream on our mini vacay, Eric and I looked into each other's eyes and just smiled. We are so in love.

Rich intimacy isn't instant when you say your wedding vows. Trust, closeness, and security develop over time. I looked across the table to my Partner in Life and thanked God for this man—his unceasing assurance, his steadfastness to love me through thick and thin—a bedrock of support unlike I've ever known.

We drove home and I thought to myself of the huge challenges I was going to have to face there.

It was Saturday, November 12. A week ago, I'd been in the hospital, bouncing off the walls, but also struggling to come to terms that I'd wound up back in the hospital somehow.

Bipolar and Pregnant

But the date also meant I was a day "late". I'm quite regular with this, but a day or two late isn't outside the norm for me. I had already had a pregnancy test at the ER and we'd used prevention since a few days prior to the ER visit. I wasn't pregnant.

But I've also been rather skinny the past few months. I'm 5'9" and weigh 115lb. When my thyroid became overactive during the summer, and D5 hit, with its Total Appetite Loss, I lost weight, and I hadn't fully regained it. Also, the past several weeks I'd begun lifting weights and rowing at the gym, and I noticed I was developing some upper body muscles on my slight runner frame. Maybe, I thought, my body fat had simply cut down too much for healthy hormone production. I'm an expert in nutrition, so I was ready to give myself a big scolding and a List of High-Cal Nutritious Foods talk. How could I have let that happen to me?

I told you I was a worrier.

Most of my life has been wonderfully boring. My entire youth and young adulthood was spent in competitive swimming. Hardly anything exciting or jarring ever happened. When I was twenty-three, my life was turned completely upside down. But before then, there was only one week of crazy mayhem I can remember.

When I was twenty-two, driving to work in my beautiful new blue 3-series BMW—sport package, special Harman Kardon sound system, a delivery truck driver was texting on the freeway and totally missed the sea of brake lights in front of him, smashing into my car. My license plate—custom too, like totally of course—was in the back seat. The car was totaled.

A couple days later, I couldn't sleep at night, because my stomach hurt something absolutely atrocious. Remembering my little sister's attack of appendicitis years before, I looked online for the nearest ER.

"That girl with the abdominal pain?" the loudmouth nurse said to another, right outside my Staph-infested curtain in the ER. "Not appendicitis. Small bowel obstruction."

"Oh...shit," I heard the other guy say. In a panic, I typed in my Blackberry to figure out what that meant.

I'd had my first flare of Crohn's disease, though at this point I'd had no idea I had Crohn's disease, and it would take nearly another two years to be diagnosed and treated. I spent three days in the hospital with a nasogastric tube, very confused. The first hospital stay in my life.

Gosh, I can't even count them now.

But that cleared up with some steroids, and I drove my rental car back home to my apartment.

A couple days later, I came home in our lovely, safe neighborhood, to a police officer in my living room, taking notes as he spoke with my roommate. Her ex-boyfriend had swung by and pulled out a gun on her. Since he was armed and potentially dangerous, the police officer told us not to stay there until he was found. That didn't take long. He was on a rampage and went to another of his ex's houses. He tied the girl up in the backyard and lit her on fire. The neighbors called 9-1-1. The SWAT team came, rescued the girl, and surrounded the house. After a gunshot, they pummeled through. He'd shot himself.

A couple days later, I went to the inspection of the townhouse I'd just bought. I was so on edge that I was expecting to open a closet door and find a rotting corpse—something scary and unexpected.

Bipolar and Pregnant

That same dreadful anticipation filled me, in my overworked little mind, as we drove home from our romantic getaway.

When we were home, Eric grabbed some leashes and took our two dogs out. I went straight for the bathroom.

When Eric and I had talked about stopping contraception, I'd been pretty excited and bought a 3-pack of pregnancy tests from Amazon. I quickly ripped open the package, pulled one out, and followed the instructions.

Two lines readily appeared.

Chapter 2. Weeks 5-8

Nobody but God knows the actual moment of conception. With ovulation itself difficult to track (and I've never bothered to figure out my own timing), and with swimmers who can live a few days before fertilization, it's all really just an estimate. Further, it can take nearly a week for that zygote—which has the full set of DNA, already determining whether Baby will be a boy or girl—to implant in the uterus wall, and hCG levels don't rise enough for detection of pregnancy for another couple days after that.

There's just no way for me to know when "it happened". It probably happened just before my ER visit with the negative urine pregnancy test. It could have happened while Eric and I were driving to Springview to check me in so I could be under supervision taking New Meds to help me sleep and put some brakes on before I kept building up speed like a big ol' Hummer flying down a hill out of control and through a guardrail off a cliff, while I was singing, laughing, and talking and talking and talking.

Two of the common signs of a manic episode are an increase in goal-directed activities and an increase in pleasurable activities. So quite naturally, while sensually hypomanic, Eric and I were having sex like it was our honeymoon, and there's no telling when that swimmer leapt off the starting blocks, so to say.

But it had happened. I was pregnant.

My hands were shaking. This was not real. I was un*balanced*. I'd just gotten out of a *mental* hospital. I'd been taking medications

Bipolar and Pregnant

and I didn't know whether they were safe or totally not in pregnancy.

Eric was still outside with the dogs. I shoved the positive test back into the box and went out to the bedroom for my phone.

I left a voicemail—attempting professional, back to my Usual Self, but probably frantic and breathless—for Dr. C. I told him I'd just found out I was pregnant, was quite worried, and could he please let me know what I should do about medications.

Had I already irreparably harmed this embryo? Mood stabilizers and antipsychotics—aren't they contraindicated? I'd just had two IPA's the night before, with Eric, on our vacation. Would that hurt the baby's brain? Wait, it didn't have a brain, but did that matter? What if I was already past the point of no return and had flooded this tiny—how big or small was it?—life with toxins that would permanently alter its formation?

I was shaking. My heart was racing. I felt like I'd start crying.

Eric came back in. Lucky, my Jack Russell Chihuahua mutt, came and found me. And then so did Eric.

We brushed our teeth, and I couldn't tell him. Not when I was on the verge of a meltdown. I could feel it.

I opened the medicine cabinet for an Ativan pill—an anti-anxiety prescription Springview had sent me home with for the restlessness that remained. But wait, I thought, now panicky and needing one more than ever: Was Ativan safe?

My heart lurched up into my throat.

This was not how it was Supposed to Be. I was supposed to have a romantic dinner with Eric, come home and have candlelit lovemaking, and then share post-coital whispers of our unending devotion for each other. I'd lay my head on my pillow, feel a magical glow in my abdomen, and intuitively know I was about to be a mother.

Dude I'm just kidding. I had never once thought about how I'd feel when I found out I was pregnant. But I *had* thought about how I'd tell Eric. There were ideas for how to surprise him with the exciting news—but that was just it—I'd be excited. And all I was right now was worried. I couldn't try to surprise him and then burst into tears.

Eric came back in, and soon afterward we got in bed. We read a little while, and my phone lit up: Dr. C was calling me back.

"Hang on," I said to Eric, grabbed my phone, and went into the guest room and closed the door. With an air filter in our bedroom that makes white noise to block out the tiniest sound (which I somehow hear, even with earplugs in—I told you I was a light sleeper), I knew Eric wouldn't hear me if I said "pregnant" in there...or if I started crying.

Dr. C told me there was very low risk with lithium and advised me to take it for now. The risk for relapse if I didn't was much greater.

"Katie," he said, "please don't worry. We can talk more about this later, but I want you to know that I have many patients with bipolar disorder and other psychiatric disorders who are excellent parents. You're going to be okay."

I went back to bed and still didn't tell Eric, who was thankfully engrossed in his book.

Bipolar and Pregnant

I slept horribly. Around 3 or 4am, I got up and ate some breakfast. I wrote a card for Eric, for later, and then got back in bed and tried to at least lie still until my alarm went off.

I was running a half marathon that morning. Eric was coming to cheer, and the group I run with was hanging out afterward, with beer and cider.

"You couldn't sleep?" Eric asked, as I drove the short drive to the race. I shook my head. "You are really excited for this run, huh? I used to get like that before big games."

I just smiled. I liked running. When I moved to a new city for grad school, I found a run group and fell in love with it. I'd only been a casual jogger—3-4 miles, 3-4 times a week. I wanted to make new friends when I moved (this was right after D2 and the suicide attempts); something athletic was right up my alley.

The group was training for the local marathon. "Well," I laughed, "I could never run a marathon, but I'll run with you guys twice a week—fun."

Every Saturday, for the next 4 months until their marathon, we added a mile to the run, and it didn't take long to realize, at home in the shower, washing all the salty sweat off my skin after a long run with them in the sun, I was running a half marathon distance casually with them, enjoying conversation the whole long way. Maybe I *could* run a marathon.

I signed up. The starting line was pretty exciting. Thousands of people were packed together, about as far back as I could see. And as the 5am starting gun went off, so did fireworks into the dark sky.

I even-split the run on a course with a huge hill at mile 23, didn't feel tired until mile 20, and crossed the finish line beaming with joy. A distance swimmer in college, I love pushing myself. For longer than a minute. That was *fun*.

I also qualified for the Boston Marathon. The new wonderful friend I'd made named Miki also qualified. The following year, Miki and I flew to Beantown to run the famous marathon together.

The Boston Marathon is something special. I competed at NCAA's, the Olympic Trials, U.S. Open, and U.S. Nationals in swimming. They're all very exciting—especially NCAA's, and especially when a member of one of the Top 3 teams in the nation. The anticipation before the race, the silence of the stands as the announcer calls us up to the block, the holy-cow here-we-go burst of joyous confidence as you leap off the block with the gun is a thrill unlike no other. I absolutely loved swimming.

But I've never experienced anything like the Boston Marathon spectators. Boston is not a big city. But, boy, are they crazy about their marathon. On their New England holiday Patriot's Day, all along the way, crowds of people are lined up, cheering their heads off, a beer in hand.

I ran the historic race in a historic heat wave. It was ninety degrees at the starting line. In shorts and sports bra, Miki and I wrote our names down our arms with a Sharpie. While running the sweltering race, where I finished in like something-thousandth place, this was not like the glory days of swimming, where I was trying to edge people out to be in the Top 16 in the nation. Yet, these nutty Bostonians were cheering for me, "GO KATIE!!!" like I were in the lead and breaking the world record. It was insane, and it was one of the most fun things I've ever done in my life.

That next year in grad school, I ran all the time. I ran the Los Angeles Marathon and dropped 12 more minutes off my time.

Bipolar and Pregnant

My friends and I would hit 10 milers of trails and hills in the dark before work. I'd run roads and golf courses for 16 miles on Saturdays like it was nothing. I loved the relationships, the discipline, the personal challenges. Running had most of everything that I enjoyed about life.

So when I married Eric last year and moved to a new city, I immediately joined a great run group. I hadn't run so much during my clinical internship year, so the two half marathons I did a few months after marriage were a few minutes off my PR. And then D5 hit.

I still can't talk about that episode of depression, at its worst in June and July. It's just too soon. Suffice it to say, I couldn't run, and I've only barely picked it up again. I love the endorphins, I love the friendships, but, at this point as I'm writing this, in the 2nd month of my pregnancy, I believe I'll never love the race like I did before.

So when Eric commented on how excited I must be for this half marathon, I just had a laugh to myself. I couldn't care less about the race. All I could think about was how overwhelmed I felt, and how I was going to pull off telling Eric about the baby without seeming as troubled and confused as I was.

I ran ten minutes slower than my PR, and we skipped over the beer and cider (oy, pregnancy) and went to the same restaurant where we'd had our first date for brunch.

I was nervous, but I could still eat. Over a shared strawberry shortcake, I slipped him the card I'd written him that morning, telling him about how thankful I was for him. How he'd been there through so many bumps in life with me, and how I knew he'd always be there through anything. How I loved him.

Then I told him to close his eyes, and I placed the positive test in front of him. He was gushing. Seeing him excited, I actually felt pretty excited too.

I'd decided that whenever I found out I was pregnant—if I ever did—I'd want to tell everyone right away. I understand that many women want to wait until after the first trimester, when miscarriages are rather common. But I also know that a miscarriage can be a very big emotional loss, and I know I couldn't bear to carry that privately. I'd want friends and family to share in the joy, and share in the loss, if it were to happen.

Most of this personal decision comes from a fear of feeling all alone and heartbroken, just like I was all alone during D1 and D2, having not told anyone about my unrelenting dark depression. Being helpless and alone are also core ingredients of trauma, and I'd do anything to avoid feeling like I did when I was utterly alone after my friend raped me.

This past D5, I told some friends about what was going on—mostly friends from church. They loved me like family and visited me in Springview. I did my best to open my heart to them, and they showed so much compassion towards me that I don't think I could have survived without them.

I know I couldn't have survived without Eric.

But I cringe to think about D5. Let's move on.

Eric and I called our family, texted friends, and everyone was very happy for us.

It was only until nighttime, when I closed the Kindle, popped earplugs in my ears, and hugged my stuffed bear to my chest that I worried. Excitement is contagious. But when I'm all alone,

Bipolar and Pregnant

I have the time to think about all my fears, and I was anxious for a long time before I fell asleep.

Did I really have the stability of mind to be a mother? What would happen if I had to be hospitalized with a child to take care of? What if hypomania, or, who cares about hypomania—what if *depression* came back during pregnancy? How could I really take care of a baby when I couldn't even take care of myself?

Here's why bipolar disorder is scary, my Dear Diary. Bipolar is lifelong. I've heard it even tends to worsen over time. I know in many people it is chronic. It is often repeated crises, over and over, of losing one's mind. And yes, though depression and hypomania aren't losing touch with reality, I really do lose my mind in them. I'm not myself in them. And with depression, I'd much, much rather be dead. The idea that this is a lifelong problem that I will have to fight till I die has me utterly overwhelmed.

So to think about adding a baby into my nightmare seems like a horrible thing for this little life who needs a mother.

Eric and I talked more about my job. It felt right to resign. The next day, I talked with my HR contact. We discussed a severance package and a separation agreement that satisfied us both, and I went to her office to sign it. That would be my last week of work.

After a hypomanic episode, I was at high risk for a relapse—into depression. Part of the reason why my hospital stay at Springview for the hypomania—which wasn't causing such a huge disturbance in my functioning, I thought—was rather long (nearly a week) is because my doctor there Dr. Douglas, a white-haired man with round eyes that always seemed to be looking into mine much deeper than a chart note's level, was concerned about bringing down the euphoric mood and rushing thoughts too fast. If I had continued to escalate, I might have crashed into a long, dark depression. But if I had been hit too hard with the medications he gave me to slow me down, I could have slid down there, too.

I understood this, when Dr. Douglas explained The Plan to me the next morning after I'd been admitted to Springview. Dr. Douglas had helped me for over a month in the summer, and we had a good rapport. I trusted him.

But after I was discharged, I felt inadequately educated on bipolar disorder. Dr. C recommended a great book for me. A lot of times, I'm scared of what I don't understand. I think back to when I read Judith Herman's groundbreaking book on trauma — one of Lindsay's assignments for me. It made a huge difference in how I understood PTSD and the less clinical problems I had with trust and intimacy.

The week after I was discharged, it was really difficult to grasp that I didn't just have recurrent episodes of depression. I knew little about bipolar disorder, but I knew enough to know that the treatments are very different, the courses are often different, and the potential for disabling loss of life are different. I was really upset.

It had also taken many years to grip that I would probably have to be on the lookout for depression episodes the rest of my life. I'd read somewhere that, after three episodes, you're almost certain to have at least a fourth. Things didn't bode well for my future, then, having had five.

What about preventing manic episodes? How in the world was I supposed to do that?

I'd only known two people with bipolar disorder before—a girl a few years younger than me named Callie who was in and out of treatment with endless relapses and hospitalizations, and Daniel.

Bipolar and Pregnant

Although they both had Bipolar I, and I have Bipolar II, the diagnosis Bipolar Anything is apprehensive enough. With these examples ever present in my mind, I was dejected.

I also felt like a total failure giving up my job. I believed it was the right decision for me, but it felt really bad. After all, I took that job in particular for my mental health. It was low stress and gave me a consistency and steady pace to my week, to keep me out in the world and active. Essentially the job was an antidepressant. And I let other opportunities that were more challenging—more like the Katie who I was in college, with huge dreams and no limits—pass by, believing they weren't the best for my health in the long run. Now, I couldn't even manage an Easy Job.

I looked online for an OB to make an appointment with. My last exam was about four years ago, aided by the use of benzos to help me not freak out during the appointment. The one before that was about six years prior—not long after I'd been assaulted. With horrible PTSD, I'd mustered up the resolve to get examined and request an STD panel then. I benzo'd up before my appointment and was relieved that everything was OK.

And by everything OK, I meant nearly nothing was OK. But at least some things were.

So, no, I didn't go looking for an OB-gyn the moment I moved to this city after marrying Eric. I'd need to find a doctor now, though, because I had to do all the Right Things for this future Baby.

I found a doctor someone had recommended to me. After making the appointment, set for 8.5 weeks pregnancy, they required me to have my PCP refer me in their system, a woman named Maureen I'd only seen once, only because my city's major healthcare system requires you to have a PCP in that system if you're going to see other doctors in it. I wasn't fired up about seeing a PCP when I wasn't sick, but I did need a gastroenterologist when I moved here, so I went in and saw Maureen just as a stupid hoop to jump through.

I sent Maureen my OB referral request. When I came home from work, stressed to the hilt about the last couple days at my job and the shock of all these new curveballs, I noticed a voicemail on my cell. Maureen had gotten my request and, apparently noticing I was taking lithium in my chart, she left me a wonderful scolding in the form of a good chewing out about taking the drug in any trimester in pregnancy.

Dr. C and I had already discussed the risks—approximately 2 in 1,000, of fetal heart defects associated with lithium. I decided the low risk was okay for this short term, before I transitioned to another drug called Lamotrigine ("Lamictal"). Lamictal is a mood stabilizer that usually works well for Bipolar disorder—especially Bipolar II like I had. But it takes a while to safely titrate up on it to a therapeutic dose, so Dr. C had planned to increase the dose slowly per guidelines and taper down off lithium to transition the drugs. It seemed reasonable. Plus, from all I've gathered the past year with Dr. C, he's a very thoughtful and thorough guy.

I'd also just read about medications in pregnancy; that very morning, I'd read the statistics. So I believed she was misinformed.

That didn't keep me from being shaken up and worrying in bed. What if she was right? What if I'm not taking this seriously? Was I mentally On Track, or was I deceiving myself? Was I unfit for all of this?

Bipolar and Pregnant

The next day, I looked back to the guidelines Dr. C—who I'd decided to trust—had written for me in taking lithium and titrating up Lamictal. Our Plan.

And then I submitted a New Patient request online for an initial appointment with a replacement PCP.

Two days later, at maybe the nadir of my self-esteem, I saw a perinatal psychiatrist, Dr. Hillary Hanson, for an appointment I'd booked at Holly's suggestion a couple of months ago. Since then, hospitalizations, medications, diagnoses, and stage in the pregnancy planning had all changed, obviously.

Dr. Hanson seemed to know a lot about medication safety and pregnancy, and that reassured me. She was also concerned about the high risk for postpartum depression I'd face. I had already read about that and was very concerned too. My book said that the postpartum period of any mother is the absolute riskiest time for a relapse—that 80-90 percent of bipolar patients not taking medication have a relapse. As if I needed any more resolve to stick with meds.

Dr. Hanson asked me tons of questions about my psychiatric history. My anxiety was very high throughout this whole interview, my spirits very low. It didn't help that the doctor needed to discuss which hospitals I'd need to be admitted to depending on what trimester I was in, if I had another bipolar episode, as if it were a routine, matter-of-fact prescription.

"I'd like you to come back and see me in a month," she said. "But before you go, I'd love for you to join our research study."

She handed me a set of pages of a research consent form, and showed me the signature line on the back page. I couldn't think about the process of being tracked during and after pregnancy by strangers for their research study.

"How about I take this home to read, bring it when I come back," I said, thumbing through the pages.

"It'd actually be easier if you could please just sign it now while you're here."

I used to comply with anything and everything. I'd do anything to make someone pleased with me. I didn't know how to stand up for myself, yet I loathed myself for it all the time. Therapy taught me so much.

Now, I hate pushiness. The angriest I've ever gotten at Eric was after he'd said during an argument something like, "Well too bad because you're just going to have to deal with it," about some situation I was upset about but couldn't really change. (That's as nasty as my beloved husband gets.) A few years ago, put me in a corner and I'd just freeze up. Now, I whip out the big gloves and pump myself up for a knockout.

It's a common reaction for trauma survivors, I've learned. Sometimes I feel the essential need to exercise my autonomy and control. I recognized I was overreacting to this doctor's perceived pushiness—that I was making a big deal out of something small. But I felt a surge of resolve, feet planted, and it felt empowering.

"No thanks. I will take it home. And bring it back if I sign it."

I got up to leave, and Eric followed.

"Oh!" she said, as I was walking out. "Congratulations. I forgot to say that."

Bipolar and Pregnant

It took me a moment to know what she was talking about. If she'd ever asked me how I felt about being pregnant, those wouldn't have been her choice of words.

Eric followed me out, straight past the appointments desk.

That night, I prayed to God. And right now, I'll tell you what I said, hiding behind a pseudonym. I told him I'd read that about one in five pregnancies end in miscarriage. And I told God it would be okay if that happened.

I'm a Christian. Maybe you don't believe the gospel, and maybe you don't even believe in God. But I talk about my spiritual life because I consider that my relationship with God is the most important thing about who I am.

I believe God knows my heart, soul, and mind, inside out. I know he already knew I was scared, that I didn't think I could handle this. Why do I beat around the bush in prayer? What I really wanted to say is I'd be relieved if this pregnancy didn't exist—if it all just went away and I could get a sense of control over my life without too much changing all at once. I wasn't ready for this, and couldn't he see what a nightmare situation I was in?

Why can't I trust God will take care of me, even with bipolar disorder?

Faith is a gift, but it also must be exercised. The Bible talks of faith both as something given, but we're also commanded to take hold of it and use it. Faith for me, that night, took on an active decision. I know my faith will waiver. It'll be easy some times, nearly absent others. But right then and there, I was going to trust God. He allowed me to get pregnant. Wishing I were in a different situation and refusing to believe that with him I really could be okay wasn't being the bold and victorious person he wanted me to be. Humbly telling him about my fears was what I needed, to receive the confidence from him I'd need to get through this.

I was going to be open with God, I was going to tackle my trust issues with God, and I was going to stand up and make decisions that were positive and that I was proud of, for me, for my marriage, and for Baby.

Week 6 of pregnancy, I had one of these decisions to make. A hiring manager in my field called me to see if I wanted to interview for a position I'd have totally killed to have. Unlike the former research coordinator job, it was a Dream Job.

I'd also found a cool part-time swim personal trainer opening at a posh gym that sounded really fun and had gone ahead and interviewed for it.

The problem with the Dream Job was the same as why I'd decided to resign from the university: I didn't think I could be a dependable full-time employee. And if I had a crisis at the Dream Job—and I feel like I'm at greater risk for having one now since I've just had one—I might burn a big bridge and make a rip right through my resume.

I don't like the idea of going on maternity leave the first year in a new position, and I'm also nervous about morning sickness. I've only had a little bit of queasiness so far, but what if I start puking my lights out and can't get out of the bathroom? And, as this Dream Job is quite inflexible, how would I ever be able to attend all my upcoming prenatal appointments? Take the rest I might need for myself and my baby?

The Dream Job wasn't sounding so dreamy.

Bipolar and Pregnant

The part-time job sounded like a better fit, until I learned at the interview I'd need to be there at 4 something in the morning. Getting up at 3 something in the morning didn't sound appealing, and after hearing from Holly and Dr. C and Dr. Douglas at Springview, and after reading about it in Dr. C's recommended book, I knew sleep was the most important lifestyle factor in maintaining remission. If I had to, I could set up a sleep schedule of going to bed at 8 every night to make the job work, but I didn't have to. Financially I don't need to work, and my social functions in the evening are more important to me and my mental health than a temporary part-time job.

The importance of maintaining a regular sleep cycle had me thinking about the start of my big hypomanic phase two months ago. The all-nighter I pulled on the red-eye flight is apparently a common trigger for others' manic phases too. No more red-eyes for me.

But what about a screaming, crying baby all night? It's wonderful that I can protect my luscious eight point five hours of sleep right now, but what about when the baby wants to feed every 90 minutes? Aren't all new parents sleep deprived? For weeks and months on end?

I decide not to pursue a job. I will take on the exciting projects I envisioned while on my manic high, and I will take care of my health. I will structure my days. This will be okay.

The day after I'd made my decision about work, my mom and her husband came to stay with us for Thanksgiving. Part of me really wanted to tell her about the whole bipolar thing, but I didn't tell her. It was still so new to me that I couldn't handle any explanations of something I was having trouble explaining to myself. Plus, I didn't want her to worry along with me. I have some super sensitive antennae that pick up others' anxiety, and

I'm already overwhelmed enough by my own. I'd crumble if I added any more. So I kept it to myself.

I keep so much to myself.

Week 7 came pretty quickly. The baby is the size of a blueberry. It gets new hands and feet, with arms and legs, this week, plus a liver, pancreas, and the beginnings of an intestine system.

I'd be pretty sure this really wasn't happening inside me, except that the queasiness has picked up, and I feel a bit pukey if I don't eat every two hours. I've been packing a few Ziplocs of pb&j's with me wherever I go. I can't remember the last time I actually felt hungry, but I have to eat to stave off morning sickness. It's okay—I'd rather feel a bit full all the time than nauseous. Statistically, I have it easy, so far. In this regard, at least.

I also have confirmation I'm pregnant because I'm so dogged tired, now in Week 8. I feel that same fatigue as when you're fighting a bad cold. I usually have good energy and am quite active, but every afternoon lately, I crave a nice lie down. Late afternoons, I've been dragging my laptop and a book up into my big warm bed or onto the sofa with me, Lucky curling up at my feet. And once I'm here, when Eric gets home, it's hard to want to get up and go out like we usually do.

The fatigue reminds me of training at altitude. As a senior in high school, and as a sophomore in college, I got to attend some special swim camps at the Olympic Training Center in Colorado Springs. At 6,000ft above sea level, there's just not as much oxygen to breathe in, to pump to your cells' mitochondria, desperately using every bit of it they can, to make energy and enable your muscles to keep firing, as you swim back and forth, high on the water like the swimming badass you are.

Bipolar and Pregnant

I never felt like a badass when I finished those first workouts in the pool in Colorado Springs. I felt like a tired wimp, possibly coming down with mono.

That is what the second month of pregnancy feels like.

Right now, on high alert for an onset of another mental health crisis, I'm seeing red flags whipping through the wind left and right, and they're unsettling. The desire for my bed when it's not sleep hours. Disinclination for social events in the evening. Chronic fatigue. All clues I've written out, highlighted, and circled before in my When Katie Gets Depressed manual, which I rely on a lot.

Seeing red flags of depression early on is crucial. In my first back-to-back episodes several years ago, I waited so long to get any help that by the time I finally saw a doctor, I felt like I was chasing the downward spiral faster than home sellers were trying to sell their houses in the great big market collapse a couple years prior. It was out of control.

It's good that my antennae are up for these warning signs. But I'm trying to be reasonable too. Talking this out with Holly, I know these are similar signs of depression, but I believe I really can attribute them to being in the first trimester of pregnancy, where exhaustion can be much greater than the fatigue I'm feeling. Being honest with myself, I don't want to go out at night because I'm just physically tired, and this conflicts with my desire to see people. When I'm depressed, I really don't want to see people, and I'll do anything to avoid them, having enough energy or not.

When I actually pan the landscape of my mood the past four weeks, since I was discharged from Springview, it has been pretty good. The anxiety has been a lot higher than usual, but my mood has actually been pretty steady.

And I'm sleeping well. Disturbed sleep—not getting adequate sleep consistently—is not only a strong risk factor for a relapse for people with bipolar disorder, but it's also the Number One warning sign for me. With depression, I wake up early, long before the sun rises, and can't fall back asleep. These are the very darkest times, where dread and despair flood over me, and torture me for what feels like an eternity. With hypomania, it took a long time for me to fall asleep, even with over-the-counter sleep aids like Benadryl. I slept fewer hours, but had more energy than usual.

Thinking about the differences between depression and hypomania, I think the widest difference between these poles is in my very first thought of the morning. With depression, the moment my mind stirs awake, before I recognize I'm conscious, or what time it is, or what day lies ahead, I have the same thought—almost as if whispered in my ear by a phantom who is not me: "I want to die." Naturally, it's hard to get excited about the day when that is the first thought you have in the wee hours of the morning.

My first thought when I woke up hypomanic? "YESSS!!!" Followed by, in rapid succession: It's DAYtime!! Winning! Can I get a party in the house??

Neither of these thoughts is happening when I wake up. While feeling like life were a party would be nice, I'm happy to reach the end of this second four weeks of pregnancy as my Usual Self.

I wonder how long it will last.

Chapter 3. Weeks 9-12

In many areas of life, I was a late bloomer. In other ways, I was distinctively not.

For example, I started taking college classes at the age of 13. I called myself a homeschooler, took all my classes at our local community college, and essentially skipped 8th-12th grades. That'll grow you up real quick.

As I've mentioned before, I also behaved like an adult professional with my sport. I took swimming very seriously and followed rigorous training with a regimented sleep schedule, understanding that sacrificing many of the carefree joys of youth would hopefully enable me to one day be the champion I dreamed of becoming in the pool. I had mature attitudes and determination that I look back on with admiration.

But in other ways, I was a bit behind the pack in life. Skipping high school didn't give me as many of the usual opportunities to date. I had my first real kiss years after all my friends—when I was 19, probably an answer to one of my dad's prayers that I stay his little girl forever, God bless him. Ah, that first kiss…

I won't tell you the kisser's real name—we'll just call him Matt. But I will tell you what happened. I'd had a crush on Matt ever since I saw him at a swim meet when I was in college. Matt turned his flirt on, and I loved it. After NCAA's my freshman year, where I'd dropped even more time than I had at my conference championships, my team rounded off the season by competing at U.S. Nationals. Matt was there.

It was the last day of the meet. I'd developed a love for mile, and I swam it that day. Because I wasn't ranked in the top 8, I swam the race at the end of prelims; only the top 8 swam at night. I went on to drop more time in the mile later, but, at this meet, I was very pleased with my finish time and was extremely proud of my season. I'd joined a team with an amazing legacy and had been given a scholarship because my coach saw potential in me, and I was having a blast, training harder than ever before and living up to the expectations we both set for me.

There was a break between my mile and the start of finals, but not long enough to go back to the hotel to rest. That night, I was anchoring the team's medley relay with the freestyle leg. My coach told me to find a quiet space in the natatorium and lie down for an hour. The mile takes a lot out of you, and it's always really hard to turn around for the power sprint of 100 meters for a relay; a nap is a great restorative help.

The natatorium was a world-class facility that had hosted the Olympic Trials before, and it had a big diving pool that had a stairwell to the diving platforms behind the main natatorium wall. Looking for a dark space that was relatively quiet, I eyed that stairwell and grabbed my earphones and parka. I passed by Matt on the way, and we just smiled. I climbed up the stairs to the 10-meter platform, high above the competition pool, tucked back, my quiet space.

I lay down, my muscles relaxing. I didn't feel like I could fall asleep, but I knew resting quietly was important anyway. Probably listening to Coldplay in my earphones, I didn't hear Matt walking up the stairs to me, until he was by my side.

"Hey," he said. "Whatcha doing up here?"

"Resting," I said, doubtlessly blushing.

"Yeah?" He leaned forward and kissed me. I kissed him back. For a while.

That night in finals, Matt broke the American record in the 800 meters, and I false-started our relay on the exchange. It hadn't entirely been my fault; honestly, the butterflier glided too long into the wall and then made an awkward last stroke, screwing up my timing — which we'd trained to be within hundredths of a second. But technically the error was mine.

Usually I'd have felt horrible for this. I was on a team of champions, and it was always an exciting privilege for me to be on a relay. But, amazingly, I cut myself so much slack that night. I was just so happy. Besides, I felt like I'd played a part in that American record.

Part of having my first make-out session late in life was also because I hit puberty late. I had a pretty good attitude about being stuck in a kid's body while all my friends bloomed, but after such a long time with nicknames like "Pancake" and "Trainer" (bra), I felt left behind. When I was fifteen or sixteen, I think I grew seven inches in one year. Trainer had fun being the new long-legged girl, finally with a proper need for a bra.

I was a late bloomer with some other milestones too. I didn't try alcohol until I was twenty, and I never had sex until I was twenty-two. Eric and I married after most of our friends already had — at age thirty-one.

But these were all things I'd looked forward to — rites of passage and stages of life. Being diagnosed with bipolar disorder at thirty-two, when the average age of diagnosis is only twenty-five, was something I'd never expected and would have obviously never wanted.

The past few weeks since my diagnosis, I've been so discouraged about it that I haven't taken a step back to see any reasons why I might be better equipped to handle it than I've thought. But this week, Week 9 of pregnancy and 6 weeks after my hospitalization, I am feeling thankful that I'm a late bloomer for bipolar disorder. And this is all because of my meet-up with Vanessa.

Vanessa is a classmate of mine in the "Philosophy of Existentialism" class I'm taking for fun at the university where I was employed. It meets once a week, and I missed a lecture the night I checked into Springview Hospital for my escalating mania. When I emailed my boss the next day saying I was sick in the hospital, I also sent an email to Vanessa, with whom I'd traded notes before, telling her I was out sick and would she mind sharing her notes with me.

The next week, when I saw Vanessa at class, she gave me her notes and said, "I hope you're okay. Do you feel better?"

I could have just said yes. I am usually very careful with what I do—and mostly don't—share with people.

"Oh, I'm totally fine. I'd been having insomnia, and it turned out to be, like, maybe hypomania or something... But trust me, I feel totally fine. So..."

Crap. What was I doing?! I started to begin backtracking, but Vanessa smiled, knowingly.

"I have bipolar disorder. I get it. Sounds like this is new?"

Floodgates of relief washed over me.

My picture of bipolar disorder had been Callie and Daniel. Callie, with on-again, off-again stability, and Daniel, whose

Bipolar and Pregnant

bipolar disorder was terminal. This normal-appearing college student didn't remind me of either of them.

I asked Vanessa if maybe we could meet after class sometime and talk, and she was glad to. We set a date. This week, in Week 9 of my pregnancy and our last day of the class, we went to a trendy café beside the campus and swapped stories.

Vanessa is only twenty. She had to sit out last year from school because her mental illness got so bad. She'd had some mild episodes of depressions first, but she was younger than when I'd had my first depression—she was only in high school.

Vanessa had a period of escalating mania her freshman year of college. She stayed up for over 72 hours, did some really bizarre and dangerous things she'd never in a million years have normally done, and her parents found out and were very concerned. She started feeling better, promised her parents that would never happen again, and then the next semester the manic episode was much worse. She saw a doctor, was diagnosed with bipolar disorder, and came home to live with her parents.

Her whole life had come crashing down.

She asked me about medication experiences, and it felt really good to talk with someone about this. I don't know why, but I'm embarrassed to need a mood stabilizer. It's so ridiculous, but whenever I go to the drugstore, I don't look the pharmacy clerk in the eye.

Vanessa told me she'd also tried some of what I'd been on, plus some others, but had ultimately decided that she didn't want to be on medications.

"So, you don't take anything at all?" I asked.

"Nope," she said. "My doctor was not too happy about this when I told her."

Something twisted in my gut.

"But, I have to do what's right for me," she continued. "And I don't feel like those meds are right for me. You know, if I'm wrong, then I'll find that out later. But for now, this is what's best for me."

I focused on dipping my rosemary French fries in the organic ketchup and eating them one by one, while everything in me wanted to turn parental on this young woman and tell her what everyone had stressed was by *far* the *most* important thing about staying well: staying on medications.

I looked up at Vanessa, and I was filled with compassion. She was so young. Though she'd been diagnosed longer than me, she didn't have the long years of awful experience I'd had with the highs and mostly severe lows of Bipolar II. I didn't want her to have to go through the pain I'd been through, with unpredictable crashes into devastating despair, to help me to be willing to do anything to prevent those from reoccurring.

I was somber the rest of the evening.

Bipolar disorder is a biological illness that is not curable. But it can be effectively treated. Before the introduction of lithium, disabling relapses were the norm. Now it is possible to live a healthy life. Sure, there are often some breakthrough episodes, but these are mostly less severe than if off medication. People with bipolar disorder can enjoy remissions—even long remissions.

Bipolar and Pregnant

Staying on medication is a real challenge for many. First, when you feel well between episodes, it's easy to believe you don't need meds anymore. I've been there, done that, with an SSRI for depression.

Second, unlike the medication Lamotrigine I'm taking, which has had no noticeable side effects with me, many drugs for bipolar disorder can have really unpleasant side effects. My friend Callie had told me about hers all the time—she gained a lot of weight, and she felt sluggish, inside and out. Psychiatry is hopeful for the development of new effective drugs that limit the side effects. But, for now, avoiding them is another reason people ditch their meds, especially during those periods of wellness which can trick you into believing nothing is wrong.

Last, you have to consider how alluring the highs of hypomania and mania can be. Those three weeks when mine was escalating, before it started turning sour, were probably as a whole the best three weeks of my life. I mean that sincerely. Imagine the feeling of a Really Great Day, when something incredibly happy or exciting happens, and those feelings like you're on top of the world. The world is your whole Frickin Oyster. That's how hypomania feels. So I really do understand why someone would take the risk and chase the high.

And this scares the crap out of me.

The day I was discharged from Springview last month, I met with Dr. Douglas.

"Dr. Douglas," I said, "This hospital stay…I've seen a lot of the same people I saw this past summer when I was here for depression. And they're not staff. They're patients."

Dr. Douglas, as an attending psychiatrist at Springview, has to see this so much. Recurring episodes in patients he has sent home on the recovering side must bother him, frustrate him, and, maybe, break his heart.

"How can I be sure I never see you again?" I asked, with a smirk, though inside, my heart was heavy.

He repeated what I'd already heard—that staying on medications was essential for maintaining remission.

"I understand this," I replied. "All of my intentions right now are to stay on medications. But you know my track record with taking them," I said, referring to the three times I'd quit taking medications when I wasn't feeling depressed. This had been a topic of more than one of our conversations over the summer when I was there for D5. "How can I protect myself from…myself?"

It's a scary thing to not trust yourself. Especially when you've always been someone as self-reliant as me.

I had serious conversations with my support team after discharge—with Eric, Dr. C, and Holly. I'd talked myself out of prescriptions before, and they knew it. I was asking them to hold me accountable, and I was begging them to talk sense into me, if my mind played tricks on me that I didn't need to take medications anymore.

It was also the main topic of my family meeting with Holly and Eric this week, during Week 10. I openly discuss my therapy sessions with Eric, and he wants to know how to help. We had loosely talked about having a family session with Holly to talk about family planning a couple months ago, because Eric and I thought we'd eventually want to have kids. Now that I'm pregnant, Eric was interested in hearing tips and discussing our concerns with an expert he's come to trust, too.

Bipolar and Pregnant

I feel good about the plans for now. Things are going well. I know it may seem in this journal on bipolar disorder and pregnancy like I have a lot of undesirable drama in my life, but I should tell you that mostly, things are okay. My day-to-day life, even with so many more appointments than I'd prefer, is steady.

The Baby has grown to the size of a grape. Next month, we should be able to hear its heartbeat at the OB's office. I bet this will be exciting.

Speaking of OB, last week in Week 9 I had my first appointment with her. Overall, it didn't go so well.

I met with Dr. C the following day. When I was in Springview with tons of energy, I made a handy spreadsheet in record speed, to help me track hours of sleep and medications I was taking. I have continued the spreadsheet, and I print out the rows of data between appointments with Dr. C and bring it to him. He said he focuses in on the sleep column.

"You didn't get much sleep the night before last," he noted.

I've started to learn that it's so much easier on me if I just jump right to the chase. If there's something I don't want to talk about, I might as well get it over with.

"Yes, I had a lot of anxiety that night because the next morning was my first OB exam. I hadn't seen an OB-gyn in a long time, and I was nervous," I said.

"Okay. How did the appointment go?"

"Mostly well," I said. I could have just said it was fine, but this guy is on *my* side, right? "My interview with the nurse was fine…"

Eric had come with me. We went to Greta's office, the nurse who will help take care of me throughout my pregnancy. She asked me a lot of medical history questions. It started to feel like a job interview. When she asked about health conditions, almost all of which I didn't have, I felt confident and like a good fit for the job. When we started talking about mental health, I felt like I was exposed for being a bad fit for the maternal job.

Eric and I had read up on what to expect at the first appointment. I feel uneasy unless I make informed medical decisions. I'm quite cautious. Looking back on my recent Springview hospitalization, the fact that I readily took new medications without questions or concerns just shows how altered my mood and thinking was. I was not my Usual Self.

I told Dr. C that they ran a whole bunch of blood tests, and that seemed to go okay too.

I knew I'd get a full pelvic exam by the doctor at the first appointment. Greta had confirmed that when we first started our interview, too. I had told myself it would be okay, to ask the doctor to tell me whatever she was going to do next before she did it, and that I would take long exhales and spell out in my head the colors I saw in the room if I felt panicky.

But we never got that far. I waited for the doctor, in the frigid room, in my stupid paper gown. What if I had a panic attack? What if I started crying? I wanted to curl into a ball and pull a giant quilt over me, dark and safe. Dread consumed me.

I quickly changed clothes. I was sweating. But still shaking.

The doctor knocked, and I stood up. I never know if I look as fearful as I feel.

"I was wondering – Could we do the exam at the next appointment instead?"

There was no sign of hesitation on her face.

"Absolutely. That is perfectly fine. Whenever you're ready."

She sent me off to my battery of blood tests, and then I went home.

And I cried.

I had to Get It Together. For the baby.

As I've said before, I've had lingering PTSD problems ever since being raped, nearly ten years ago. I don't really like any physical exam. I have to coach myself through something as simple as a doctor listening to me breathe with a stethoscope.

I've definitely improved. I don't panic anymore, and I'm hopeful that one day I won't even feel uncomfortable. But pelvic exams are different. I doubt they'll ever be okay.

That afternoon, Greta the nurse called me. She said she'd like me to come in and see the team's social worker. I told her, as I had in her office that morning, that I already see a therapist regularly. But she said they'd like me to see someone familiar with the whole team. I was too embarrassed to ask why, so I scheduled the appointment.

Now I *really* felt unfit for motherhood. Maybe my ideas aren't accurate; my perceptions may be wrong. But two years ago, when I interned in a GI clinic in another city, it seemed that problem patients were the ones who saw the social worker. The ones who couldn't Get Their Shit Together. The ones who had compliance issues or had too much personal drama to have effective treatment. The ones who needed someone to help them get together the basics of being a Responsible Adult, to make sure they weren't just wasting the doctor's time.

I knew this wasn't me. I am responsible. I am informed. Every test and procedure Greta talked about in our interview I had already researched. I understand every stage of fetal development now, and I know what I should and shouldn't be doing to take care of me and my baby during this first trimester. And I'm doing it all.

Except. Except my mental health problems prevented me from going forward with that beneficial first physical exam. Except I got out of a locked mental hospital last month and have a list of these hospitalizations on file now. Except I have the blaring diagnosis of bipolar disorder screaming its warnings, front and center of my medical chart.

I felt humiliated, typing the appointment in my calendar. Katie McDowell: unstable, unbalanced, unfit.

And then the clincher came.

Two days after my OB appointment, I looked up my blood test results in an online patient portal. CBC = great. Thyroid hormones = normal. Everything was looking good. And then I opened the syphilis screening test.

Positive.

My heart skipped a beat. Syphilis?! I tested positive?!

There was a note by the results saying the lab was automatically sending my sample for a second different test—one that helps confirm the diagnosis. I totally panicked. I picked up the phone and called Eric, who was driving to work, and I rapidly began

Bipolar and Pregnant

some internet research on these blood tests while I breathlessly told him I—and now we—might have an STD.

This is the part of my journal where I'm going to shift gears into the Very Personal domain. I mean, I've already brushed the surface of vaginas and uteruses, and I've told you a smidgen about my sex life. But now we're going to talk about my attitudes and beliefs about sex. You're probably going to disagree with a lot of my mostly faith-based beliefs. Please don't judge me. I promise, I don't judge you.

I have major hang-ups with sex. Many times, after having pleasurable sex—and even during it—I feel dirty. And not just a bit icky, but deep down, through and through, disgusting. Many times, after sensual love with my amazing, devoted husband, I feel used and violated. Our first couple months of marriage, I'd escape quietly to the bathroom and cry. Many times, my reflex when my husband shows physical affection is a startle response, and my heart beats quickly, and my throat squeezes tighter.

I fully understand *why* this is. I understand trauma. But it still hurts. It still gets me down. Sometimes I feel inadequate.

Sometimes, I feel fundamentally ruined.

To drastically complicate the picture, the word "guilt" used to hover around sex for me. I lost my virginity at age twenty-two to someone nearly twice my age, and I wasn't proud of this. The power dynamic was inappropriate: he was my boss.

A million times worse, he was married.

I also understand how this happened. A late bloomer, I was maturing sexually and everything in my body wanted to explore. I spent a lot of time with someone I admired tremendously, and when he started giving me special attention, I was enamored. It's a tale as old as time.

Some people might say that though the context wasn't exactly appropriate, it was a natural exploration, and there must have been so many beautiful outcomes to this young love experience. I navigated my sexuality in a consensual relationship, and no one got hurt.

But that isn't true.

As I've said before, I'm a Christian. My belief is that God meant for sex to only be inside the covenant relationship of marriage. I believe there is nothing dirty about sex, and, within agreement in the marriage, absolutely anything goes. It's meant to be tasty, luscious, sensual, erotic. And even when it's blah, boring, and otherwise not wonderful, it's still a way to bring two people intimately together. Sex is good.

But I believe sex outside marriage is wrong. I'm taking God's Word as serious, and if God says sleeping with a married man is wrong, then I believe my relationship and having sex with that man was wrong, no matter how right things felt and no matter how much fun I thought I was having. And I knew it was wrong. I did it anyway, and then I felt the unbearable weight of guilt.

Very shortly after this relationship ended, my friend raped me, and I carried all the profound guilt I had into that. I believed it was my fault, and everything about sex felt shameful.

This isn't completely gone.

Several months after being raped, I knew I needed to get right with God, about the affair I'd had, and all the other little lifestyle choices I'd been making that had made that relationship feasible.

Bipolar and Pregnant

It is true that believing the Bible and holding your flawed actions against its standards can incur a guilt that might otherwise nicely evade me. But, more importantly, my faith also gives me a way to erase that guilt with assurance.

With a broken heart, I confessed to God, and asked for forgiveness. I'll briefly explain my whole Christian faith in a nutshell. I based my prayer on the faith I have that Jesus was my substitute, atoning for every awful thing I would ever do, and that God remains faithful to forgive those who trust in Jesus's sacrifice as the only atonement that can ever be made to please a perfect God.

I know I am fully forgiven with God. That doesn't mean I don't have to remind myself, often, regarding various failings. I know God wants me to enjoy the freedom of forgiveness, so that I'm not held back in anything in life.

But sometimes keeping regrets off my back is easier said than done.

So when I saw a positive result for syphilis, I felt guilty, and quite ashamed.

I ran through every possible scenario of how I could test positive. My first thought was that maybe it's a mistake. Maybe the result could be a false positive. I hoped.

I also wondered why I didn't test positive back many years ago, after I'd been raped and had asked the OB-gyn at my routine appointment to run an STD panel. ...Or did I only ask to check for HIV? Now I couldn't remember.

I know Eric didn't pass this to me. He is in the military reserves, and he gets tested for everything under the sun routinely. If his last blood test had been drawn after we got married, wouldn't he test positive? Or was his last test before then?

I'd never before developed any sores or the rash on my hands and feet that I saw online as the beginning symptoms of infection—symptoms I would, as a self-diagnosed hypochondriac, notice and call medical attention to. So I couldn't have it, could I? Or was it simply dormant—a latent disease just waiting to show up?

I went back and forth with possibilities. According to what I read, syphilis is very rare now in the U.S. Not all, but most of the people who contract it have sex without condoms, which I interpreted as risky and promiscuous.

"I've never been risky and promiscuous!" I thought, frustrated and upset. I hadn't even ever had sex without a condom, until I married Eric.

Even when my friend raped me, he took the time to put on a condom, one knee jabbed just below my ribcage, to keep me from getting up. I developed Crohn's disease around that time and had some painful gastritis. When the pain came, I had flashbacks of this moment, so strong that I'd have convinced myself my pain was all psychosomatic, had I not seen the endoscopic images of my diseased GI tract myself.

But, even after all my hopeful arguments as to why the test had to have been wrong, ultimately, it still was possible it was right. My stomach knotted tighter and tighter.

I called Greta.

"Greta, I'm worried about my blood tests. I tested positive for the syphilis screen." I cringed.

"Oh we see false positives. Do not even worry about that. And even if it is a true positive, you'll come in and get a shot of antibiotic, and you'll be fully treated. No harm to Baby. Anyway," she said, swiftly moving on like this was Absolutely No Big Deal, "I was also going to call you about your blood test. Have you been told you have low platelets?"

Medical issues are a bit fascinating to me. When I was in grad school for Nutrition Science, I was most interested in aspects of disease and nutrition, and I found myself doing much more in-depth background medical reading. I thought about becoming a physician, but my interest faded the more and more I considered my strengths and what would truly be the best fit for me. I decided that nutrition counseling—more of a coaching role—was the right track for me. But I added to my then regular reading of TMZ (I'm not proud of this) *The New England Journal of Medicine* and other medical journals. I keep up on a lot of new medical advances, and I'm still learning more about illness.

Including mental illness.

Anyway, I have a harmless but unusual issue called pseudothrombocytopenia, which is the appearance of low platelet count, but, actually, there is no problem with my platelets, and I have the right amount. Mine simply clump together with an anticoagulant in the tubes they react to, and only a small number of my platelets get counted. So I always get this false test result.

I reassured Greta and told her I still had the medical note from the hematologist who investigated this peculiar problem. After explaining my results, calmly and competently, and assuring Greta that it was okay and I'd go back and get another sample using a different kind of vial, I hung up.

Wait, what had I been worrying about? A blood test result my clinician had assured me was likely an error and swiftly treatable if not?

I saw Meg, the trauma therapist I'd begun seeing several weeks ago, that afternoon. I had wanted to talk with her about how I couldn't go through with my OB's physical exam, but that could wait until later. I told her about the positive screening, and how I'd walked through every possibility of it being correct versus incorrect.

"Are you worried that the antibiotic wouldn't work if the results come back positive?" she asked me.

"Oh no, it's definitely curative," I said.

"But you're still anxious?"

I was totally anxious.

And, honestly, it had nothing to do with syphilis. Yes, untreated, syphilis can be very dangerous. It can infect your central nervous system, cause paralysis, and even death. It's a very serious disease. But I wasn't at all worried about that. I know antibiotics work.

I stepped through the doorway of the discussion she opened, and we talked about sex. My struggles with guilt, my struggles with shame. How if I had an STD, I was meant to drag along my regrets.

Again, I faced what I believe as an unshakeable fact that God doesn't hold my regrets against me. And I don't need to either.

So when Greta called the next week in Week 10 and again in Week 11 to tell me that both of the more specific blood tests

Bipolar and Pregnant

came back as negative—I didn't really have syphilis, I was glad, but I know in my heart I wouldn't have been upset if it had truly been positive. I had found peace before the results, either way.

Later in the week I met with the OB office's social worker. To my liking, the appointment was short and sweet. I was glad that apparently I hadn't been singled out as a potential Big Problem but that everyone with any history of mental illness met with the social worker in case problems came up during and after pregnancy. When she learned of my great support team, she pretty much congratulated me on my proactive use of support and gave me her card for if anything came up as an emergency. I decided I had a different perception of social workers and patients who see them. We're not all Unmanageable after all.

Speaking of support, I just went to my very first support group, with Eric. The fact that I've had a [repeatedly debilitating] mental health diagnosis for nearly a decade and have never tried a support group alludes to my attitude toward their potential helpfulness. My thoughts about support groups are admittedly steeped in ignorance. I shouldn't attempt to give a real opinion without trying one, but here are my thoughts, nonetheless.

If you're reading a book on bipolar disorder, there's a good chance you're already familiar with it. Maybe intimately. If that's so, you might have the case where you or a loved one has benefited from a support group. I don't believe they're not beneficial for anyone. I just have found reasons that have kept me from trying them, and you can feel free to mentally argue with each of my points you disagree with.

For starters, I worry that they're the blind leading the blind. I'm sure support groups give wonderful encouragement to one another, but I bet advice sneaks in there too. I'm very careful with whom I choose to be on my support team. Trusting their advice has come slowly. I've always avoided online discussion forums, and the first thing I check on any article is whether the source is reputable. I'm leery of strangers in a support group.

Also, I'm afraid a support group would slow me down. Maybe I shouldn't apply this mentality, but I can't help it: I think to be my best I need to train with the best. This is what was engrained in me very early on in swimming. I'm afraid that who I really should get to know are the people who are doing so well they can't even be bothered going to a support group.

Last, I really don't want any more reminders in my life that I have bipolar disorder. I think about it every time I take the elevator up to Dr. C's office in some anonymous business building, every time I walk the pathway, usually green and blooming but now grey and still with winter, to the old yellow house on the corner, now converted to therapy suites, where I meet with Holly. Every single day since I was diagnosed at Springview, I enter my bipolar medicine taken into my spreadsheet. I feel like I have enough reminders and enough awareness and that, while I'm symptom-free, I should just go Enjoy Life Being Symptom-Free.

"It's just like how I relate with Crohn's disease," I told Eric, driving over the rolling hills, our seat heaters on, our cold hands thawing as we sped away from Springview, where the support group was held. "It's hard to be in a group when I'm not identifying with the illness. I could never be in a Crohn's support group, because aside from my infrequent flare-ups, it's as if I don't even have it."

Eric was a dear to come with me. He never hesitates to do anything supportive for me. We went because someone personally invited me. When I was in Springview the past summer, one of the support group leaders came and introduced us to their mental health association, and he gave us a copy of their quarterly newsletter. I noticed they had a poetry section

Bipolar and Pregnant

that took submissions, so I submitted a poem—one that I wrote right there in Springview Hospital, depressed and wishing for suicide.

The newsletter editor published my poem. So, the next quarter, I submitted another one—right after my Springview release for the mania. She published it again, and she invited me to come to the association's holiday party, held right before the support groups.

I fully expected the party to be four or five people standing around with Styrofoam coffee cups. Instead, I was surprised to open the door and find the room filled with dozens of people of all ages, cheerfully milling around tables of food, a few in holiday costumes, some festive music playing.

After the little gala, everyone broke off into their respective support groups. I chose for us the "Maintaining Stability" group. With our brief introductions, going around in a circle, I learned that of the fourteen in the group, thirteen have bipolar disorder.

Eric was the fourteenth person.

The discussion topics varied widely, from light boxes for the winter, to boundaries with family over the holidays. I never said anything, but I listened.

After the whole light box discussion had finally died, Lorraine, a small middle-aged woman who kept her eyes mostly on the carpet, spoke up.

"I came here to work on getting back my stability. I've just had another episode." Depression, clearly; it doesn't look nearly over. "I don't know why it happened. I got remarried recently. Maybe the changes… Man, it's been twenty years since my last episode, and this is really hard to deal with."

People gave her encouragement, talked about changes and stress, and Lorraine's eyes slowly moved off the floor to meet ours.

"I know you're doing so well now," Eric said, helping me make the correct turns as I drove. Eric knows the route home from Springview by heart; he visited me almost every day for a month in the summer. "I don't think you *need* to be in a group. But I'm glad we went tonight even if we never go again."

I was agreeing, thinking I wouldn't go back, unless maybe I started to feel like my supportive friends were on a completely different plane than me, as happens when you are depressed, and your friends are not. That's what had been helpful about our somber groups in the hospital—I sat in a room, feeling so hopeless, believing that I could never relate with anyone, and at some rare, beautiful moments, I did relate.

The helpful moments were never profound. And often the encouragement came from an unlikely source. Over the summer, with D5, when I'd been at Springview about three weeks and was only just starting to begin to think that *maybe* I wouldn't *always* feel this horrible forever, I was in one of the daily group meetings. A burly guy named Bob was talking.

"I don't know, man. I just got so depressed. Couldn't keep up in work—had to cut back my orders cause I couldn't get to all of 'em. And, Gah, I'm so pathetic lately." Bob shook his head at himself. "It's like I'm so lazy but I can't do anything about it. It's like—I wash my clothes, and then I bring the basket up to my room, right? And I just drop it on top of my bureau. Can't even put them away. A slob. So pathetic."

Bipolar and Pregnant

We all let Bob take a breath. Maybe he had more to say. In the hospital, nobody talks on top of other people. People don't tend to talk, anyway.

But then, on the other side of the room, a younger girl looked to Bob and said softly, "Wow. You still do your laundry?"

When I went to the kitchen for lunch after that, I sat down by that girl. We didn't talk. I didn't need to.

"Twenty years..." Eric said, in the car. "Twenty!"

He was talking about Lorraine. As I was listening to her, all I could think of was how awful she was feeling. I know Depression intimately. There's nothing worse. But Lorraine, who could have been the biggest downer of the whole night, turned out to be the most encouraging. Maybe maintaining stability was possible. Lorraine, with bipolar disorder, like me, had gone twenty whole years without an episode.

I'd be grateful for just one.

Christmas came in Week 11. Christmas, with all of its delicious food everywhere you turn. I have had no trouble eating and am gaining about a pound a week. I feel good. My lower abdomen is definitely thicker, and my boobs have totally doubled. That's not saying so much, but the point is: my body is beginning to grow and reshape for pregnancy. For some reason, this makes me quite proud.

We decided to stay local for Christmas. Eric and I went out and did our own romantic staycation on Christmas Eve, and then we went to our favorite couple's house for Christmas Day.

New Year's fell on a weekend, so Eric and I drove to see my little sister Aubrey and her family, who live a couple hours away.

Katie McDowell

Aubrey and her husband have three kids—a two-year-old, and twins aged one. They're adorable, and I think it's really fun to see my little sister as a mother of three.

Aubrey is very different from me. She has neat talents and a strong personality. Unfortunately, growing up, I don't think these were celebrated. Many authority figures compared her to her older sister—me, in an unfavorable way. I realize as an adult, it must have been difficult to have me as a sibling. I was a perfectionist who always aimed to please. Maybe I'm wrong, but I think this was a large part of why we usually didn't get along at home. This is sad, because, with all our parents' fighting, it probably would have helped us to have been there for each other through it.

Now as adults, our relationship is much stronger. We text each other pretty often, and we've both matured into being much kinder and more flexible with one another. I think we appreciate each other. And now I admire her.

It feels really good to be the little sister in the life stages and look up to Aubs, who went off to live in another country after college, get her PhD, get married, and have three kids. For some reason, I love turning to her for advice—relationship advice when I was dating Eric, and now pregnancy advice, seeing as she's pretty much a pro at this.

We had a wonderful weekend with them. The kids were non-stop. A toddler, and twins! They must be chronically exhausted. I could never manage.

I'm now closing out my 12th week. Next week I have my first ultrasound with the OB. I'll hear the heartbeat, and I'll get to see the first image of my baby.

God, please let it just be one in there.

Chapter 4. Weeks 13-16

I saw my baby today. Right there, tucked below my belly button, moving his tiny little arms and legs, heart beating 163 beats per minute. He's really in there.

And it's just one. Phew.

Of course I don't know whether it's a he or a she yet. But we'll know that pretty soon.

Today I went to the genetics counselor at the OB's office, with Eric. She explained the blood tests I had opted for—the standard ones offered to everyone that help predict risks for chromosome abnormalities. Then, Eric and I went to an exam room, where a woman with an ultrasound was waiting for me. I lay down on the table, slid my jeans down low, lifted up my shirt, and the woman spread warm gel on my abdomen.

I've had a few abdominal ultrasounds before. In the ER with a Crohn's small bowel obstruction, some sensible physicians consider the high number of CT scans I've been exposed to already and instead order a simple series of X-rays, and sometimes an ultrasound, to help rule out problems with peripheral organs. These ultrasounds I've had have always been very painful. There's nothing worse than some dude jabbing a transducer in your gut while it feels like it's about to burst. And there is nothing interesting about these ultrasounds; the images on the screen are completely unidentifiable to me. I simply try to do random math in my head, made complicated by the Dilaudid I've been given, to distract myself till it's over.

"We probably won't be able to make out anything," I'd told Eric, walking down the hall to the room. "But hopefully they'll take some still shots and point things out."

As the woman held the transducer and looked at the screen, Eric and I turned to watch too. I was perfectly comfortable, ready for a boring view of unrecognizable layers and quadrants of flesh.

But right when she pressed onto my abdomen, the very clear outline of a baby appeared. It was surreal. I've been aware that I am pregnant, growing something inside me. But I never pictured in my mind exactly what that looked like. To see a tiny little human moving around inside of me was startling.

And pretty cool.

The nuchal translucency—the layer of fluid at the back of the baby's neck—was measured. This measurement helps to predict serious birth defects. Baby's was normal. I'll hear back on whether the blood tests were also normal in a week or two. Hopefully there are no genetic defects.

Growing up, I thought I had good genes. Though I didn't understand exactly what these were, I equated them a lot with my swimming abilities. Sure, I trained exceptionally hard and took full responsibility for my swim times. But when I noticed that I excelled in my sport naturally, noting other girls around me who also trained very hard but couldn't advance like I did, I had to make a space of gratitude for something within me that wasn't up to me. I'd been imprinted with something special, I thought.

Swimming ran in my family. My brother and sister were also highly competitive swimmers, both as well competing with scholarships for top-10 Division I universities. Though my dad hadn't been a swimmer, he had also been a very good athlete.

And, at six-foot-five, the passage of his genes to our swimmer frames didn't hurt. My athleticism was certainly at least somewhat genetic.

Parents can feel responsible, in an unfavorable way, for the genes they pass on. For example, my mom, who was five-foot-one, and had strong musical talents—not athletic—felt left out of contributing to our genetic inheritance in sports. So it was a great joy for me when I learned and told her that my mitochondria—likely the *most* important cellular attribute anyone could ever pass on to me, I explained—came entirely from her; the genes for the powerhouse of the cell that made the energy critical for being a distance swimmer come only from the mother. She liked that.

In my youth, I also thought of good genes as being physically attractive. I've generally liked and never had a problem with my appearance, perhaps minus being Pancake still at age fourteen. Each of my parents had no trouble maintaining a healthy weight, we all had good complexions, we all had straight teeth, nice hair, et cetera. We were never going to be picked to be on the cover of a Ralph Lauren catalog, but I've always thought we're a pretty good-looking family.

When I learned more about chronic diseases, I figured I'd hit pretty lucky genes too. Nobody in my family has diabetes. There's been some heart disease in older relatives, but I attributed it to dietary choices. There's been some cancer in grandparents, but I figured smoking probably was the main cause. My parents, now in their sixties, are totally healthy. So, I always thought that nothing runs in the family, as they say.

I developed Crohn's disease in my early twenties. I know this has a pretty strong genetic component, but no one at all in my family has had IBD—just me; I haven't thought of it as an inherited disease. Along with this autoimmune disease, I recently developed Graves' disease too, where I produce antibodies that basically over-stimulate my thyroid. Again, no one in my family has ever had this; this doesn't seem to me to be genetic.

It wasn't until my diagnosis of bipolar disorder that I recognized a hitch in my DNA.

Bipolar disorder has a strong genetic basis. The concordance rate for monozygotic (identical) twins, who carry the same genes, is very high at 80%. Genes don't explain everything, but they do explain a whole lot.

I had a grandfather with bipolar, I have an uncle (grandpa's son) with it, and I have a cousin (uncle's daughter) who domino the lineage. This makes me just a stone's throw away, apparently not far enough to escape its snare.

I don't think my genes are so great anymore.

With the genetics counselor, we discussed disorders that, while extremely severe, are also exceedingly rare. I was quite distracted. There's only one genetic illness I'm afraid of passing to Baby.

Bipolar disorder is polygenic—there are multiple genes involved, but even with a much greater diversity than the matched alleles of twins, the risk of first-degree relatives sharing bipolar disorder is 10%. There's a 10% chance my child could live life with bipolar disorder.

To make matters far more gut-wrenching to me, the literature shows that, on top of this 10%, there is an even greater likelihood my offspring will suffer from major depression—adding up to a one in four chance of living with either depression or bipolar disorder.

Bipolar and Pregnant

Am I cruel for conceiving?

The next day, I saw the OB Dr. Greenberg and had my first full exam. Greta took me to an exam room, took my weight, and asked me a bunch of questions. Then she told me the doctor would be in soon. She didn't hand me a paper gown when she left.

The doctor came in and talked with me. When it seemed like she was wrapping up, I asked, "Are you doing an exam today?"

"We can if you're ready. But we don't have to."

"I am," I told her. Not avoiding her eyes, I said, "I took an Ativan before I came here. I don't intend to take another one in pregnancy. But it has been a long time since I've had an exam, and I wanted to be sure I'd get through it."

Dr. Greenberg nodded.

I added, "I expect the next ones will be a lot easier."

I knew I had to stop taking the Ativan I was on in the hospital for my manic episode and had continued taking, though on a much lower dose, for the few days following discharge before that pee stick. It's not very dangerous, but it does increase the risk of facial deformities, and taking it before delivery can cause the baby to be born lethargic. And if the mother took it regularly, the baby can go through benzo withdrawal at birth. I've been through that twice, so any warnings against benzos I take very seriously.

The exam was so easy. She voiced everything she was doing, and it was over very quickly.

I felt really good about getting through it. I'm not upset for needing something to help me relax. Remembering what I learned from exposure therapy years ago, it's good for me to challenge myself with fears, but not to a point where I'm overwhelmed. Now I have confidence that next time I won't need any help.

If you've had a baby, you might be wanting to give me the 4-1-1 about all the intrusive exposure during labor and delivery. You don't need to; I already know about it. But that is six months away, and right now I can conquer what I can conquer, and hopefully I will be prepared for that day when it comes.

I'm now rounding out the end of the first trimester! All in all, mine was quite easy. I read that the easiness of my queasiness puts me in the top 15% of lucky pregnant women; most have it much worse. And my energy is back; I'm running my usual workouts with my run group. I'm a little slow, but I feel good again. Everything has gone very well.

People always want to know, "Have you had any food cravings?"

No, I haven't had any food cravings.

I just crave beer. An ice-cold IPA, right from the tap, or straight from the bottle. I'm not a big drinker; just one drink is how I prefer things.

This isn't the case for many people with bipolar disorder. I read that over sixty percent of bipolar patients also have substance abuse problems. Oftentimes, alcohol and drugs are used to help dampen down manic agitation and alleviate crushing depressions. Other times, manic highs manifest both very poor impulse control and an accelerated drive for potentially dangerous and exciting experiences—a perfect storm for substance abuse.

Substance abuse isn't only an effect of bipolar disorder, though; it also can incite and exacerbate episodes. Mood-altering drugs—and certainly the disruption to sleep patterns they tend to have—can devastate the weak mood regulation capacity in bipolar patients. I treat alcohol cautiously, and I know there are times when my depressions get so bad that I must avoid it entirely.

But for now, I miss a good craft beer. How many more months again?

It is now mid-January. This is a time of relative stillness. People have returned back to their schedules, afresh from vacations, with a renewed sense of focus. Maybe they want to start spending more time with their families. Maybe *less*. But whatever the aim, there is a noticeable shift. People talk of resolutions, and there's something special about dumping last year's desk blotter in the garbage and replacing it with a big white clean slate. Change is possible.

I love personal goals. I thrive on them. Most of my goals are specific and measurable, but my New Year goals are purposefully not. I make aims, and I'm my own judge of my progress. For example, two years ago, in my clinical internship, there were a couple tedious projects I was putting off—rushing to meet deadlines. I didn't think this was typical of me, but I surveyed my life and noticed other ways I procrastinated. "I still have a week to pay that parking ticket." "I know I'm passing by the dry cleaners, but I don't feel like going in—I'll get my dress next time." I wasn't missing deadlines or actually falling behind, and I kept good lists, and things didn't slip through the cracks. But, still, this wasn't the person I wanted to be.

I decided my 2015 aim would be to stop procrastinating. I used the holiday break to catch up and then get ahead on my work projects. Then I knocked out most of my big to-do list (which had a lot on it—I was also planning my wedding), and I handled things as they came up. I've kept this up, and it's a very freeing lifestyle change I made that I'm proud of.

When 2016 started, I decided on another goal that suited me: I would investigate all of my questions. How many times in a week do you catch yourself wondering things? Well, I wonder about facts all the time—from something as simple as what the actor's name is for a movie I'd just seen, to what the half-life of regular Lamictal is compared to the extended-release version. With my miraculous iPhone, I'm always learning, and my 2016 aim will hopefully always stick with me.

This year, my aim is relational, and it's mostly for my marriage. As I've mentioned, Eric and I have been learning how to have healthy conflict. I'm a peacemaker who fears conflict. Often I suppress any anger and try to end our struggle ASAP, meanwhile harboring quiet anger I'm not even aware of, which of course makes it hard to feel close. My aim now is to become adept at noticing anger—towards anything—and thinking through why I'm angry and what would be the best thing to say or do about it.

I've been working on emotional awareness ever since I saw my first therapist, nearly seven years ago. I used to have a debilitating inability to name whatever I was feeling. I grew up in a family that never discussed feelings, and where really only pleasant ones were acceptable. So when PTSD hit, with all of its floods of panic, shame, and the despair of my first depression, the only way I could describe my emotions were with "bad" and "overwhelming". Therapy has taught me so much. For over a year, I brought to therapy a list from a book that simply had several dozens of emotion words on it—my cheat sheet to draw upon while we were talking.

I have made some wonderful improvements. Maybe you can sense from my journal that I'm not so much at a loss for words for how I feel about everything that's happening. This isn't always the case on my own, but, right now with weekly therapy, I'm doing okay at articulating. This journal is a tremendous therapeutic aid, too.

A helpful way for me to know what I'm feeling is being aware of my body. I'm quite skilled at interoception in sports. I had a natural feel in the water for kinetic efficiency; I had exceptional technique, to help make up for my limited strength and power. I was very good at using biofeedback for strategic pacing in my long event, the mile. And I've pretty naturally translated this into pacing for the various distance races I now run for fun.

Emotions are different. But, likewise, I try to pick up on physical cues—that my heart seems to beat a bit fast and my throat closes just a bit when I'm very anxious, that my stomach seems to twist and I hunch over just a little when I'm disturbed or confused, and how my arms have a subtle swing and my chest faces out to the world when I'm feeling spirited.

But there's one emotion that I still have problems with. It's hard for me to notice it until it's too big to miss, mostly because I don't want to notice it: Anger.

I grew up with a parent who didn't know how to control their anger. In a torrent of rage, they would repeatedly hit me, and, in response, I learned as a child how to dissociate when this happened. I have forgiven them for this, and they've changed. We have a very good relationship now. Though I don't think this was required for my forgiveness, I even understand how this happened in them. But, since there was never any room for me to express anger, and because anger seemed like a very volatile and dangerous emotion, I have always repelled it out of fear.

When I think of anger, I also think of being raped.

I don't know the exact date of when that man took my dignity and shattered my spirit. But it was this month, ten years ago.

Here in Week 13 is my tenth anniversary of being raped.

I told this to Meg, at the end of our last session. Next time I see her, I want to somehow honor the time. The time I've lost, the life I've missed, and also the compassion I've built and the strengths I may have never otherwise known. Post-traumatic growth, they call it. Maybe Meg and I will talk about that next time, but for now, I want to tell you.

I was raped. By a friend. What seemed to me out of nowhere, he tried to kiss me, and I backed away. Embarrassed for the both of us, I told him he had the wrong idea. Then he got forceful. It felt like he was *angry* when he pushed me down, grabbed my wrists and held them over my head. I tried to get up, but that was futile. I'd been trapped and powerless like this countless times before, so I did what I'd always done.

I gave up.

I wasn't even angry. In fact, maybe also because he immediately apologized and held me as I cried, I let him keep contacting me and allowed him to come over, again, only a week later. It's astounding, but I think I wanted to be sure he didn't feel horrible about what happened. When he again made advancements and I turned him down, he ignored me. I disconnected most of what was happening, and I don't remember being scared. This made me very confused afterward. On one hand, I *knew* I'd been raped, and I demanded he never contact me again. I was a

Bipolar and Pregnant

complete wreck of emotions and knew this was related to what all happened and that I couldn't tolerate ever seeing him again. But somehow I wasn't angry with him; I felt very ashamed and blamed myself.

And I didn't tell anyone.

When I finally got help, I learned how to make it through the overwhelming tumults that pulled me in and down, where I could hardly breathe and life became unreal. It took me many weeks just to write down and say aloud what had happened. I talked about it over and over, and the strong physical reactions in my body reduced over time. A lot of time. Over years, the unthinkable happened: I became able to talk about being raped without crumbling—now often even without strong emotions at all.

That doesn't mean its effects are gone. I haven't had nightmares or flashbacks in several years now. But I do still have visceral memories that can evoke very powerful emotions. It feels like my breath is taken from me if my hands are above my head, lying down; I automatically panic and pull them down. I can't stand anything touching my neck—a cape snapped too tightly at the hairdresser's, or a scarf wrapped too close. But the worst is if anyone grasps my wrist.

I have healed, but I also have not.

I also struggle with anxiety in a more generalized way. I think— at least I hope—I'm good at hiding this. But hypervigilance is my default. It's hard for me to ever fully relax. My muscles seem always tense and ready to fire. And I hear every noise. It's as though my ears are constantly scanning for a sound. This is exhausting sometimes, but I've had ten years to get used to it.

Katie McDowell

The one thing that gives away my anxiety—that chronic current of adrenaline that moves through me—is my startle response. It's so strong that I always have people profusely apologizing for scaring me so bad as they suddenly appear in a doorway, or walk behind me, or—the worst—touch me. I laugh to minimize my frustration and hurt over these seemingly permanent changes to my body, but, truthfully, sometimes I feel hopelessly stuck.

A part of me also wonders if developing bipolar disorder was related to being raped. Genes made me susceptible to bipolar, but often a major life stressor incites a first episode. My first depression followed being raped; I considered that whole awful suicidal time as being very much set off by horrible circumstances that plummeted me down to the blackest depths. What if the whole "kindling" idea is right? What if, had I never experienced that first depression, the subsequent ones and the subsequent hypomanias never would have occurred?

If I'd never been raped, would I have developed bipolar disorder? I don't know. Maybe no one can ever know.

One of the strongest preventions against developing PTSD is talking with someone about the rape soon. I waited over three years to tell anyone what had happened. I had three years bearing all of the shame and despair on my own, feeling like a ghost whose body had long since died—a phantom, hopelessly going through the motions that everyone else called life.

When I think about what happened, sometimes I feel sad, and sometimes tears come to my eyes. But the pain is bearable. It's okay for me to feel it now.

A lot of rape survivors eventually become interested in helpful activism. It is a way to continue healing and to help prevent their atrocities from happening to others. They say it's empowering. I thought that, maybe, to honor these ten years as a survivor, I'd join a cause. However, I'm strong, but I don't quite trust my footing enough to do something bold like open up to strangers, or volunteer with something like an assault crisis hotline, or anything that has too much involvement with rape at a pace I cannot control, fearing that my memories could find a way to haunt me again.

When I was raped, another reason why I didn't tell anyone is because I thought I didn't know anyone who'd ever been sexually assaulted. I believed no one could possibly understand. I felt entirely alone.

But since I've opened up individually to many friends about it, I've learned that several of them — even friends who I'd known ten years ago when I was raped — had also been sexually assaulted. It makes me wonder, if I'd known that about them back then, would I have told them? Would I have felt like maybe, possibly, there was a safe person who just might understand? Could I have avoided the three years of compounded PTSD and depression that led me to make the only choice I saw available, twice, to just end it all? Could I have prevented what still remains — how I'm still trying to heal?

For now, I can't be a leader for change in our society, where one in six women, plus twenty percent of these as men, are raped. But starting this tenth anniversary, I can be committed to being that safe person for the people I know. For someone like me.

Like all difficult anniversaries, and like all happy anniversaries, it came, and it went. And that is life — painful, intricate, changing, and, through it all and in spite of it all, meaningful.

The next week, the genetics counselor called with good news. My risk assessment came back as good as can be with the statistical tests they performed for the major chromosome abnormalities, which estimated for my baby a one in ten thousand risk. Because of this, she didn't recommend the further precise testing of the bits of Baby's DNA that are now circulating in my blood stream.

I get worried about things, but this wasn't something I'd even thought about after that appointment. And it's not because I believed I was immune to those rarities. In fact, my own brother lost his first baby to Trisomy 13; I very much know how real chromosome disorders are, and how painfully devastating. Just because I wasn't anxious to know the results didn't mean Eric and I didn't celebrate the good report, though.

Here in Week 14, I feel excellent. I don't even feel pregnant. Last Saturday I ran ten miles with my big run group, so this Saturday I planned to do another ten-miler with my best running buddy Caitlynn.

I love running with Cat. She's quite a bit faster than me and runs further than me, so we try to plan our weekend runs to where she runs a few miles before we meet, and a few miles after I finish, to give her a satisfying workout while I tag along for part of it. We used to be neighbors, and she's the first friend I made here, a few days after I moved here after my honeymoon with Eric.

Running is an important outlet to me. It's not my only outlet, but it's probably my favorite. To keep running enjoyable for me, I want to be sure I never take it seriously.

I was a serious swimmer. There wasn't anything I wouldn't have sacrificed in order to become faster. Swimming was a core part of my identity, and I loved swimming from the bottom of my heart.

The problem with running is, I know from swimming how I can turn goals into obsessions, and I'm afraid I'd lose my carefree love for running if I took it too seriously. There are other goals in life now that are immeasurably more important to me than athletic ones.

Goals like maintaining my mental health.

I like to push myself sometimes, and going for PR's is okay, but I'm even more committed to Totally Not Caring about my progress. I'm not in any danger of ever being competitive in running—I'm honestly just not very talented in it, but the effortlessness in which I, as a disciplined lover of achievements, can turn a seemingly harmless goal into cause for unmitigated compulsive devotion makes me vigilant against becoming competitive with myself in running.

I've never owned a pace watch, and I doubt I ever will. If I feel like going slow, I do. If I decide while out on a ten mile run that after only three miles I'm tired and would rather go home and make waffles for Eric and me, I divert my path and head straight home. Basically, I am careful to protect myself from myself, and let running be the healthy outlet it is for me. The endorphins, the way it keeps my body fit and strong, and the camaraderie make it something I stick with routinely and with enjoyment.

When I run by myself, I either zone out and enjoy a stress-relieving peace quite like meditation, or I mentally tackle a problem I've been facing. When I run with others, we're not talking while we're running; we're running while we're talking. There's something about movement that relaxes me and makes it easier to have deeper communication. And without needing to focus on the other person's facial reactions, there's a freeness to say what's on my mind in a way that I'd otherwise be too afraid to share. And I don't think it's just the private companionship that also causes my running friends to reveal their inner depths to me sometimes, too.

Caitlynn is many years younger than me, but she's very mature. I have a low tolerance for immaturity in grown adults. With Caitlynn, I don't even feel older than her, except that she can run really long runs on consecutive days without feeling an accumulation of fatigue. Youth gives you a much quicker recovery.

"Glad we got to sleep in this morning," Cat said of our later start time today, as we took off down the long bike path that goes for many miles. I've always liked working out in the morning like this. It gets your day started, and I have more energy and a more optimistic outlook after a good morning workout.

"Yeah, it's nice," I replied, pulling my gloves on my hands.

"I didn't get home till two this morning," she said with a laugh.

Also, Cat is able to function on very little sleep, something younger people seem better at, and something I'll never be able to do with bipolar disorder. She seems to have so much energy. I remember what that felt like. When I was her age.

And then, when I was hypomanic.

My energy has returned from the fatigue of the first trimester, and I'm back to my usual peppy self. With Caitlynn I ran at the pace I hold when I'm in good shape. And our second half was much faster than the first. I wasn't tired. I've been sleeping well, eating well, and have had a steady good mood. I'm in excellent health.

Which makes it confusing why I had to see a Maternal-Fetal Medicine aka "High-Risk" OB.

Bipolar and Pregnant

As I was leaving my OB's office earlier in the week, Greta told me that the Maternal Prenatal Medicine clinic would call me to set up an appointment. They indeed did, and now I have an appointment with a Dr. Rebekah Stein next week.

"I don't understand *why* I need to see a high-risk OB," I complained to Eric the next day over dinner at home. "I'm in excellent health and don't see anything 'high-risk' about my pregnancy."

"Greta didn't tell you why?" Eric asked.

"No, and I didn't think to ask. I just stupidly nodded and went along."

I usually come to doctor appointments with my questions ready—sometimes even written if I think I might forget. I do this with Dr. C too and write them on my spreadsheet. Do you get a sense of my MO? But when I'm confused, I don't always think on my feet because of anxiety, and I don't speak up when I need to ask my questions.

"Can you call her?" Eric asked.

But I didn't want to call her. Because I assumed I knew why Dr. Greenberg set up the consultation, and I didn't want to hear Greta confirm it.

"Well..." I trailed off, looking at my plate. "She said something about not wanting anything to fall through the cracks. But I bet they're just worried about my mental health."

Eric wasn't convinced. Greta had been pleased I'd already seen a perinatal psychiatrist, and the social worker in the office basically applauded me and signed off on me with all boxes checked.

"Maybe there's something else they're thinking about. Maybe there was a communication breakdown somewhere in the OB's office and the message didn't get to you."

That could make sense. He encouraged me to just call Greta and ask.

We finished dinner, and I helped him load the dishwasher. I couldn't let it go.

"I mean, it's not like I'm not taking care of myself," I grumbled. "They obviously don't understand that I'm not going to let anything 'fall through the cracks'."

"Yeah," he replied. "I know. You're on top of everything."

"Exactly!" I kept on. "Seeing an endocrinologist, who is tracking my labs regularly and knows all about perinatal Graves'. Keeping up with my GI doctor—and that's totally under control. And seeing Dr. C, like, all the time. Sheesh. I'm covered!"

Dishtowel in hand, Eric quickly kissed my forehead. "Totally on top of everything."

That night, after Eric had fallen asleep, I turned my Kindle off, pet Lucky goodnight, and ruminated. They were concerned about my bipolar diagnosis. They wouldn't have had any concerns if my chart still said "h/o Depression" like it always had, even though I think depression is the only part of my bipolar diagnosis worthy of any concern. They're worried I'm going to fall apart, act erratically, and be unable to take care of myself in my pregnancy. That's what makes me "high-risk" to them.

I relented the next day and called Greta. She explained that the appointment with Dr. Stein was only a consultation and that she's an expert at the overview of medical conditions in pregnancy. She said she could give Dr. Greenberg good recommendations, such as if additional ultrasounds might be necessary to track the baby's growth.

I cheerfully thanked her for the explanation and hung up.

She hadn't even alluded to mental health.

That evening I ran by myself. It was unseasonably warm for January, and I wore only a short-sleeved shirt and my running shorts—which I noticed were a little tight around the waist. I did a smooth six-miler, beginning at my usual train stop and hugging along a long stream on a rather empty trail, except for a few people walking their Labs and Golden Retrievers and Australian Shepherds, all of which I had to stop and pet.

Mental health stigma is very real. For people who don't understand mental illness, it can be a confusing matter, and sometimes people assume the worst. Character flaws, poor parenting, spiritual problems—many people conclude things like these are the causes of mental illness, as though our suffering is a consequence of poor choices. Instability and unpredictability are expected of us, and labels like being "a schizophrenic," "a manic-depressive," and "an agoraphobic" are used to help clearly differentiate us from "normal people". There is stereotyping, prejudice, and sometimes outright cruelty.

I experienced stigma right at the start of my mental health problems. During D1 and D2, I finally confided in two friends from church that I was struggling with depression. These very well-intentioned ladies explained I needed to search my soul and repent to God, because there must be a sin problem weighing me down and keeping me in despair. So I did search my heart. And in not finding relief from God, my despair only grew. I also distanced myself from the church. I couldn't handle any more of the shame I already felt.

A couple years later, one of these ladies, in dating a man with a family member with severe mental illness, wrote me the most beautiful and heartfelt apology. I'd already forgiven her in my heart. I know that mental health problems are not well understood by the general public, and maybe, sadly, even less so in the Christian community.

But Christians get depression too. And bipolar disorder.

In the throes of depression I'm already inclined to isolate myself and feel worthless. In isolation, it's very easy without the needed reminders that God hasn't changed to feel estranged from God. It feels like he left and never cared. Depression is when I need God the most. And though I don't believe spiritual problems cause my episodes, I do know that in these episodes I need extra help from others to have confidence in the beliefs I'm assured of when I'm not depressed.

Over the past couple of years, I have been more open with many of my friends, including my church friends, about my struggles with depression. Grateful to say, I have not felt stigmatized by my close circles. But I do feel they must be the exception to society at large and the other people I know who I don't feel comfortable enough to share with. I hear their voices in my head all the time, putting me down.

...But are they really others' voices in my head? Or my own?

The more I thought about it on my run, my assumption that my OB's office thought I'd be a risky case due to my bipolar disorder said really how I felt about myself. Not only was I projecting my own fears about my instability during pregnancy on my treatment team, I was also misattributing the harsh thoughts I have toward myself, deep down.

I'm inadequate, I'm damaged, and I'm innately defective.

Stigma hurts. I know this well. Because despite my loyal and loving friends, for a long time now, I've been the victim of it. With myself as my own worst offender.

Dr. Rebekah Stein and I had an excellent appointment together.

"I thought we could talk today about your medical conditions or concerns and how these could potentially impact your pregnancy, along with how your pregnancy could potentially impact your conditions."

Dr. Stein had a clean notepad on her desk as she sat across from me. She rotated the pad a bit so I could read and follow if I wanted, and she grabbed her pen.

She asked for my input on the main discussion topics and agreed mine were the ones she'd wanted to discuss too, writing down large bullets each for Crohn's disease, Graves' disease, and bipolar disorder. Dr. Stein seemed fully knowledgeable on all three of my conditions in pregnancy, and she had clearly reviewed my chart. She found my level of understanding and then matched her communication to it. She answered my questions and assured me she and her team would be available if I had any questions or had an acute flare-up of any condition.

I don't think I've ever seen a doctor like her. She wasn't narrowing in on one big problem (which I'd assumed she would and that she'd choose bipolar disorder to investigate); instead, she saw the whole of my body. I felt like she understood who I am physically. And with the respect she showed me and attunement she had with my own knowledge and concerns, I felt like she understood an overview of the non-physical parts of me too.

Why can't I see myself through her eyes, with no assignment of shame?

Now in the 16th week, Baby is the size of an avocado. It has all of its major organs but just needs to grow—which it's really about to start to do, rapidly. It can move all of its limbs, suck its thumb, and grasp its umbilical cord. It can even hear my voice now.

This week I turned thirty-three. I had a low-key celebration. There have already been talks of "gender reveal" parties and upcoming baby showers for me. I'm also the chair of my state's professional nutrition association's social networking group and have been hosting a number of gatherings and events. A simple night out for a movie and desserts with just Eric and my friend Gabriella was perfect.

We saw a PG movie I'd been eager to see, about a dog. Eric and I love dogs, but our tastes for movies hardly intersect. I love the quiet dramas—the ones that either end up winning Oscars for "Best Picture" or they go unnoticed at the box office. I also like non-violent mysteries and psychological thrillers. Eric, on the other hand, loves the flashy action movies with loads of CGI— the bigger the production budget, the better. He also prefers comedies; I usually can't stand them. I probably take myself too seriously, but it really annoys me to watch people acting stupidly silly, and instead of finding them funny, I find them a waste of time. Eric and I meet a little closer with romantic comedies, as long as the lines use wit, irony, and clever sarcasm—admirable humor, to me.

A couple weeks ago, we saw an animated movie in theaters. Yes, we really did; it was for parental training, I swear. I went along with Eric on this pick, because I'd just roped him in a couple weeks before to see a sad and grey drama. We both laughed a lot and enjoyed the lighthearted movie. But afterwards, at home, for some reason I felt obligated to read every headline article online on world politics on my laptop, followed by a publication on the history of nutrition guidelines for dietary fats for heart disease.

But when it comes to dogs, I'm just a child. I adopted Lucky from the shelter seven years ago, and I have loved her to absolute pieces since. She is The Best Dog. She has short tan fur, huge ears, a tail that can wag her whole little body, and eyes that are always looking to make contact with yours. Being part terrier, she has a lot of spunk and energy, even at age nine. Being part Chihuahua, she loves to snuggle and always wants to be near me.

The day I adopted Lucky, I put her in the little dog bed I'd bought for her, in the living room. I pet the timid little thing goodnight, and went to my bedroom and climbed into bed. Lucky came right in, looking up to me on the floor, and then emitted a little whine.

"All right, little Lucky," I said, and retrieved her dog bed, bringing it in to my room, right beside my bed. I stroked behind those ears, kissed her little head goodnight, and went back under my covers. But Lucky hopped right out of the dog bed and repeated her staredown and whine routine.

I smiled. "Poor little Lucky," I told her, picking her up and gently placing her on my blanket. She found her way right up against my side, curled up tight, and sighed, eyes closed.

And that was the end of that dog bed.

I adopted Lucky during D2. The hospital I was in following my suicide attempts had me fill out some "safety planning" worksheet. I'd been thinking about getting a dog, so I wrote down that getting one would be helpful for my depression and panic problems. I actually followed through with the idea when I went home from the hospital. Lucky has been a lifesaver; it's me who's the lucky one.

With D2, I was able to go to work, but barely. I had atrocious concentration problems and was having daily panic attacks. Always afraid I'd have one with an audience, I kept myself hidden in my office, and I brought as much work home with me as I could. I couldn't bear to be around people. On weekends, when I didn't have responsibilities, I was hopeless. There were days I set the singular goal to go outside and get the mail, and there were days I failed at this.

There were also quite a few weekends when I took a whole dozen Benadryl in the morning. I thought about suicide all the time, and finding a way to be unconscious was all I could hope to do. I know this sounds disturbingly dangerous. But in the frame of mind I was in and with no other coping skills in my life to just get through a day, these sleep-a-thons probably saved my life.

Cutting myself probably also saved my life. I discovered this amazing relief on accident with a nick to my finger with scissors. Plagued by ongoing dissociation, cutting myself grounded me and made me feel real, instead of the ghost I was then during most of my existence in the world.

Cutting also soothed me when I felt panicky. In the seconds it took to grab the piece of glass I kept under my sneaker's insert and make a small slice at my hip, just enough to draw beads of red fluid, my throat opened up, I breathed deeply and fully, and the room stopped closing in on me. It was far more powerful than Xanax.

Bipolar and Pregnant

But even more addicting.

Holding Lucky gave me, and still gives me, this type of relief. When I feel unreal, as always happens during depression, looking into Lucky's eyes and petting her soft, warm fur makes me know I'm really here. And when my anxiety rushes up in the day, or when panic wakes me up in the night, she gladly lets me pull her close, and I focus on the rise and fall of her little blonde belly as she breathes, her slow and steady rhythm bringing mine down to match hers. Sometimes this ends with me falling into some small sobs into her neck, my tears on her fur.

Even when I feel like I can't move—I can't get out of bed, I can't feed myself, I can't bear to let my skin feel the world outside, I care for Lucky. She has never missed her walks, has never missed her meals, and she has never missed my tangible love for her during my episodes. I've taken care of something outside myself, even when myself I cannot take care of.

In the summer, Springview allowed me to go outside in their big park with Eric for some time in the evenings. Most of the time, Eric brought Lucky. I wished for suicide all day long at Springview. I felt as though I'd never connect with a person ever again. Not even Eric. Even Eric felt distant and unreal, in a whole different world, and I could never cross the chasm. But I felt connected to Lucky.

I know that Lucky is an animal, though she's loyal and adores me. But Eric is my soulmate. Eric and I love each other with a passion; our hearts, bodies, and minds are becoming one. There is no one on earth I love more. And yet, depression destroys attachment, and the only living thing I feel any attachment to is, inexplicably, Lucky.

If I can't feel attachment to Eric in depression, what will happen between my baby and me? What if he feels completely unreal to me? What if I can't bear to see her because I feel so estranged from her?

I'm preparing to be a good mother by taking care of myself—particularly my mental health—in pregnancy. I'm keeping up with my medicine, with my appointments with Holly and Dr. C, and I'm sticking with a healthy sleep routine. I'm keeping myself nicely busy with projects that give me a satisfying sense of accomplishment, and I'm socializing with friends, writing partners, and workout buddies throughout the day. I'm doing all the Right Things.

But sometimes episodes just have a mind of their own. And I don't have confidence they won't return.

When depression hits, will I be able to feel any love for my baby?

Chapter 5. Weeks 17-20

Here in the 17th week of pregnancy, I feel excellent. I don't feel one bit pregnant. In fact, I've been feeling quite young and ...sexual.

Here she goes again about sex, you think. But sex drive is an important topic to mention here as I write about pregnancy and bipolar disorder.

Many medications for bipolar disorder cause low libido, or difficulty or inability to climax. If you've ever seen *A Beautiful Mind*, about John Nash with schizophrenia, you probably remember the heartrending scene where Nash laments to his wife that he can't keep taking his pills because he can't function sexually on them. The pleasure and relational intimacy of sex can be severely impacted by medications. Just because they may be life-saving drugs doesn't mean these side effects should be slighted.

Bipolar disorder itself affects sex. In a depression episode, anhedonia—loss of pleasure—blankets everything, and this almost always puts a big damper on sex drive. For me, in depression, there's just no appeal to sex whatsoever. But in the opposite pole of mania and hypomania, sexual pleasure is intensified.

Anonymous as I am here, I'll tell you that my sexual appetite is close to an all-time high, save perhaps during my hypomania, which also had the aphrodisiac benefit I can't enjoy in pregnancy of alcohol. Right now, I feel like I'm twenty-one in my body again. It's wonderful.

Pregnancy hormones are known to boost the libido in a lot of women. But I can't help but wonder if the switch to Lamictal, which doesn't have sexual side effects, off my SSRI, which often does, made a difference. I can't know what's causing it. For now I (um, and Eric) will enjoy it.

I wouldn't be the only one to have a muted libido on an SSRI. Sexual side effects are the most common problems with the antidepressants; many patients quit taking them for this reason. Yet, I've read that rarely do patients and their doctors discuss these side effects. That's a shame.

However, while I think it would be great if the patient-physician dialogue on sexual side effects were improved, I admit that I myself am not doing anything about it. I'm pretty creative, but I can't find myself coming up with any way of telling Dr. C that lately I've had a voracious sexual appetite, and, oh, P.S. this might have something to do with SSRI cessation and we might want to consider that in the future.

In addition to the possibility of the changing hormones in pregnancy increasing my libido, I feel a lot more seductively sexy with Eric because my body has changed. And by my body, I mean my boobs. They've tripled. It happened so quickly and noticeably that I could have easily convinced any of my close friends if they didn't know I was pregnant that I'd gotten a boob job. I like them, and I'm entertained by the doubtlessness that they're going to do anything but expand more.

I know full well that this isn't always enjoyable to many pregnant women—especially ones who don't start out in A-minus cups like me. But I'm just going to enjoy these newfound assets while they're here. We'll see if, later on in pregnancy, like when I'm like a whole foot wider and have hot flashes and kankles, I still feel so sexy.

Bipolar and Pregnant

I definitely have the start of a baby bump. This delights me. This week, I went out for mocktails with the girls, and when I was washing my hands in the restaurant's bathroom, I turned to the side to check out my little bump in the mirror. Smiling, I gently rubbed it, just as a woman opened the door and saw me. Realizing I must have looked ridiculous, I almost explained, "I'm pregnant, just looking at my baby bump." But I kept my mouth shut, hoping I contributed a little spice for her to walk away with.

Finishing up this fourth month, I have plenty of energy—not in a manic way, a qualification I feel I now must add. I ran fifty miles this week. This included a seventeen miler on Saturday—the longest run I've done in about four years. I'm not pushing my pace, and I'm fully prepared to switch to something gentler like swimming when running becomes uncomfortable. But for now, I'm enjoying the long runs with my friends. I am feeling a little inspired by them, as most are training for various marathons, to run a marathon again. Maybe spring of next year, when Baby is around nine months old.

If an episode doesn't strike between then and ruin my plans. That has happened. I was starting to train to run the Chicago marathon this past fall with Caitlynn. But then D5 hit.

I can never make any long-term plans with great certainty.

I've been spending more time lately with my friend Danielle. Danielle and I met at Springview this past summer—or at least that's the first time I remember meeting her. She recognized me there from runs she's done with my big run group, though I didn't recognize her. When she was discharged before me, I said we should swap numbers and go for a run together when I got out, but she told me she'd already given me her number back when we met at run club. I checked my phone, and sure enough, she was there.

This is how depression destroys your memory. Or maybe it's the anxiety that surges during my depressions that messes with my memory. Either way, events, conversations, and people all become blurry, and it was as if I'd never seen Danielle before.

A few weeks after I was discharged, Dani and I met up over coffee. My depression was improving. I was back at work, feeling a little more confident, and managing my daily life again okay.

Over my intensely rich cappuccino, with marvelously thick foam that I mindfully noted I was enjoying, Dani told me how she had still been having trouble. Having had resigned from her job, she wanted to find a different one that was part-time and less stressful, but she worried about being able to cope. She's been having trouble finding the right medication. She's been feeling like a failure.

I connect with Danielle.

Dani had a depression episode when we were both at Springview, but Dani's persistent struggle is anxiety. Not just feelings of tenseness or stress, not just excessive worrying. Dani's struggles with anxiety, in her body and in her mind, are crushing.

One time at a coffee date, in my first trimester, I asked her about what had been bothering me that week, as I went to see Holly, and Dr. C, and my OB. The cognitive restructuring, the deep breathing techniques, and the constant checking and rechecking for any appearances of signs and symptoms have me spinning around at a dizzying speed, and it never seems to end.

Bipolar and Pregnant

"Danielle?" I asked, glancing around and then moving my head in closer. "Do you ever just get sick of all the effort?"

Dani emitted a laugh, and smirked as she moved her head in to mine, conspiratorially. Compassionately, she let her smile die down, until it disappeared, her hands cupping the base of her hot porcelain mug. "All the time," she said.

I thought of Dani after I went to see Holly today. Two weeks ago, in Week 15, I said goodbye to Meg, and I told this to Holly.

"It was just too many appointments," I explained. "I felt like seeing two therapists was overkill."

What I didn't say is that I thought that seeing a trauma therapist was a waste of effort.

I've had a continual struggle with anxiety. Worries aren't even on my mind—it's a current in my bloodstream. In depression, it becomes severe, and I have panic attacks. But even when my mood is fine, I still have a problem with low-level anxiety, and I can't seem to shed it. Out and about during the day, I don't really notice it, but when I lie down at night before I sleep, or when I get back in bed after having to pee in the middle of the night (a most common pregnancy symptom), I feel physically uneasy. It takes me a long while before I can fall asleep.

This bothers me. Is there something wrong with my body, or is it all "mind over matter"?

I've read that over 80% of bipolar patients suffer another psychiatric disorder too—most commonly anxiety. I've also read that bipolar women are particularly more prone to comorbid anxiety and have a seven-fold increase of an anxiety disorder compared to the general population. Moreover, bipolar II patients are more likely than bipolar I to have anxiety disorders.

So my having problems with anxiety are not at all unusual to have with my bipolar disorder.

The day before I last saw Meg, I received my blood test results of my thyroid hormones. Hyperthyroidism can cause the physiological symptoms of anxiety—mild shakiness, quicker heart rate, and a general sense of being wound up and on edge. With Graves' disease, especially during pregnancy, I have to get my thyroid checked often. Because of the anxiety I've been feeling, I was hoping that my thyroid was a little overactive. But it wasn't; all my hormones were normal.

Instead of this being good news, I was discouraged, and the next day, I told Meg I needed a break. Why should I keep banging my head against a wall, when anxiety never really goes away?

A few days later, I met with Dani over bagels and iced tea while we each studied for licensure exams in our respective fields, which would broaden our opportunities. I'm making good use of my time not employed, and I always enjoy seeing Dani.

Midway through a page I was reading, I paused to get a sip from my tea, and as I looked up, I noticed Dani. With one hand holding her place in her large textbook, she used the other to dab at the corners of her eyes, as she fought back tears.

"Dani. What's wrong?"

She shook her head at herself, wiping the swelling tears.

"I'll forget everything I've read. When I take the test. And there's just too much to read."

"Dani..." I said. She apologized for crying, and I told her to please just let me be a friend. What good is a friend if you can't be authentic with them?

We'll just gloss right over the fact that I always put on my best face with everyone.

"That," I said, pointing to her book, "is one thick mofo. Looks very overwhelming."

She nodded, blinking through tears.

"You'll take it one little bit at a time. Just like you've been doing. If you need to take more time before scheduling the test, you'll take more time. Go as slow as you need to. It doesn't matter. You're going to get there."

Dani wiped her eyes with her sleeve. I motioned to her textbook again, half of which was tabbed with post-its.

"Look how far you've come already! You're doing great. Just keep doing what you're doing. You're going to get there."

Oftentimes, what we need most to hear, we cannot say to ourselves.

One of the most powerful therapy assignments I've had was with my first therapist. I was full of self-blame for the rape and felt that my suffering, which I berated myself for feeling, was deserved. My assignment was to pretend everything I had experienced had happened to a good friend, and I was to write a letter to her.

For all the pain I was suffering at that time, I didn't cry a whole lot. Like an on/off switch, mostly I was either wholly numb or flooded with panic and dread, overwhelmed. But as I wrote that letter, the page ran wet with my tears. I'd do anything to let that friend know it wasn't her fault, that she didn't have to feel ashamed, that it was going to be okay.

Self-compassion is not something I understand well; self-criticism, I'm an expert at. I also think I understand compassion for others, and I have seen strong examples in my life of this. But to myself, I mostly repel it, drowning out others' compassion towards me with my own louder, disparaging voice.

Part of the reason it's hard for me to accept compassion is because I don't have the equanimity necessary to be able to discern between the things in my control and the things that aren't. It's the essence of the Alcoholics Anonymous serenity prayer, and it's an important capacity to possess in order to rightly respond to painful situations.

When you think of a control freak, you might think of someone who tries to make all the decisions, who bosses people around, who notices and gets excessively upset at people when things don't go as expected. I can be quite selfish—I see this in my marriage. I am changing, learning to be flexible, and learning to accept—and hopefully one day cherish—Eric's preferences and ways of doing things that aren't like my own. But all in all, I'm not really a control freak so much in this sense.

But there's another kind of control freak, and I fit this bill to a T. You see, I have this ideal of who I should be. I should be endlessly loving, and I should say all the right things at the right times. I should be at the top of a career, an expert in a field. I should be able to perfectly balance work, a social life (obviously a rich and ever-fulfilling one), and a wonderful, harmonious marriage. I should be able to keep my body healthy and fit, and look good doing it too.

It would be bad enough if I stopped here with my perfectionism, but I don't. I hold myself responsible for bad things that happen to me outside my control. Like the ways I was smacked around as a child. Like my parents' ugly divorce. Like being raped by a friend.

Like having bipolar disorder.

I hope you can see why bipolar disorder is so hard for me to accept. I have had extreme mood episodes, on one pole spiraling upward towards a frenzy of uncharacteristically thoughtless behavior, on the other pole plummeting down to the endless thoughts and even intentions of suicide. Though able to still make choices and intervene, sometimes barely, these episodes have been outside of my control. And I absolutely hate to acknowledge this.

After meeting Dani for bagels that day and helping her through her onslaught of anxiety, I thought some about my own. I know I worry, and I'm working on that, but I also know that my body hasn't healed and that a lot of the anxiety I feel is lingering PTSD. I have read quite a bit now about the H-P-A axis disruption in trauma. I know in my head that this isn't my fault.

Why do I keep blaming myself then? Why do I fight so very hard to ignore my anxiety? Just like wallowing in self-pity paralyzes helpful change, continually chiding myself or refusing to acknowledge and accept a physiological problem I have is only making things worse.

I finally permitted myself to look online for a weighted blanket. These soft blankets look just like ordinary blankets but are filled with tiny beads, causing them to weigh several pounds. It provides an even heaviness over your body that to me is very calming, very soothing.

I discovered weighted blankets at Springview in the summer, and I used one again when I returned with my agitated hypomania. There in D5, one day I simply could not stop sobbing. Even on a heavy benzo regimen, my anxiety was through the roof. Still crying, I went to the nurses' station.

"I just can't calm down," I told my nurse. She knew more medication couldn't be offered; I'd just taken some an hour before.

"Wait here," she kindly said. "I think we might have something to help." She disappeared in the offices and was back a minute later, carrying a blanket.

"It's heavy," she said, handing it to me. "Wrap this around you. See if it helps."

I thanked her and went to sit on a couch. It didn't take long at all, and I was stilled. I didn't go anywhere without that blanket on me for at least a full two weeks, there at Springview.

I had planned to buy my own blanket when I was discharged. I still had anxiety and needed to take medicine for it after I went home. But I couldn't bring myself to order one of these specialty blankets. I reasoned that I'd go off the medicine, as I indeed did, and there'd be no physical evidence left of past problems.

On my laptop at the kitchen counter, I found a site to order custom weighted blankets, choosing its weight, size, and fabrics. I filled out my billing and shipping information, but when prompted to confirm the order, I just sat there.

If I bought this, would I be admitting defeat? Would seeing that blanket at home make me feel embarrassed about myself?

Eric came in, dressed in sweatpants after his shower, and looked over my shoulder.

"It's a weighted blanket," I said. "I used one like this at Springview." I was ready to exit the site and close my laptop.

"I remember that. You loved that thing."

Of course Eric would remember the blanket. That month is so foggy for me; I forget that his memories of that time aren't so clouded and unreal as mine. Eric visited me nearly every day in D5. The only days he didn't come were when I absolutely insisted he go spend the evening with friends—for his own wellbeing, I said. Not to mention the added bonus that I wouldn't feel like such a worthless burden with him seeing me.

Eric knows I've been having trouble with anxiety and that it's affecting my sleep. I probably unintentionally minimize my problems with him, but I do try to tell him everything. He knows I've been having trouble falling back asleep in the night.

Depression—and bipolar disorder, of course—can be a painful challenge to spouses, too. Eric hit a sharp learning curve when we were newlyweds when I went through D4. No matter how many times I told him that my low mood had nothing to do with him, he felt he must have been somehow to blame. This of course made me feel even worse. I tried my best to keep my suffering to myself, but this was obvious to him, put an even greater distance between us, and I felt even more isolated.

What helped us round the corner with this problem was a family therapy session. It helped for Eric to hear from a professional and someone other than me that my depression wasn't caused by him. For someone who is always racking his brain for solutions when faced with problems, it helped for Eric to learn some ways he could help.

Not only is education helpful for family members, educated family members are helpful to the one with bipolar disorder.

Family can help spot the early signs and symptoms of episodes. I am now in the regular habit of telling Eric how many hours I slept. If there are any consecutive nights of poor sleep, we've decided to review my sleep spreadsheet together, and I've agreed with Dr. C to give him a call if there are more than three or four in a row. This hasn't happened yet, but for someone who hates to feel like I'm being an annoying alarmist for bothering a clinician over something that might not be important, Dr. C's direction to phone him for this is comforting to me.

Eric and I are also in agreement that he can ask me why if I ever cancel a social engagement. With depression, I try hard to keep scheduling dates with friends in addition to my regular social calendar like my run club and my Bible study group. But I'm an expert of backing out of them when I inevitably don't feel like going. Just as I like knowing I have full permission to contact my doctor about sleep, Eric likes the security of our mutual agreement to bring up any isolating behaviors if I start showing them.

Isolation was certainly not a part of my recent hypomanic episode. But I did want to quit seeing a therapist and taking any medication. In our family session after this recent episode, Holly helped us know how to handle this if it comes up again. Given my history of quitting medication, I'm afraid that, despite my intentions now while my mind is healthy to stay on them, there will be an episode in the future when I'll believe I don't need them. We decided that, if this happens, I'd schedule a family meeting with Dr. C to discuss the option before I just quit taking them. Now, I know full well that Dr. C won't agree that it's okay for me to stop them, but if I trick my mind into believing I don't need them, I could potentially believe he might agree. And when he doesn't, I'm hoping the added insistence from the professional I've come to trust will help sober me up to reality, and at least I'll have alerted my team to help me stay the course.

Bipolar and Pregnant

Holly discussed in our family session that, while Dr. C wouldn't likely ever agree that quitting meds is a good idea, there might be—and likely will be—a time when it's quite all right for me to terminate or pause therapy. Again, in an episode it may be hard for me to objectively decide when the time is right, so Eric and I have agreed that if I ever want to quit, we'll have a family session to discuss it first.

As you can see, it takes careful advanced planning to stay healthy with bipolar disorder. You have to come up with a plan that will realistically work, and this is a very individualized plan.

Involving family with plans, like mine, requires trust. I trust that Eric won't take my signs of depression as personal failures— mine or his. Eric trusts that I'll be honest about reasons for canceling plans. And he trusts that I'll try to be open with him about my mental health problems.

So when he saw me looking for a weighted blanket online, I chose not to hide it and forego the idea.

"I think a weighted blanket would help me relax," I told him. "I think it would help me fall back asleep when I wake up."

"What do they feel like? How do they make them heavy?" he asked, sitting down at the bar stool next to me.

"Some kind of beads I think. Like heavy sand, evenly distributed on your body. It kind of feels like…a gentle hug," I explained. "It just feels…very calming."

"Nice. You should get one."

"You think so?"

"If it feels good and might help with sleep? Totally," he said, nodding. "Plus, when the baby comes, it'll probably be really stressful for a while. A blanket like that'll probably feel extra good then."

I nodded, smiled, and ordered the blanket.

Eric and I? We're a Golden Team.

Here in Week 18, Baby is the size of a bell pepper. I've had no problems, the only nuisance right now being regular bathroom runs to pee.

I saw my OB this week. Basically, the appointment went like this:

Dr. Greenberg: "How have you been feeling?"

Me: "Perfectly fine. No complaints."

Dr. Greenberg: "That's great. Any questions or concerns?"

Me: "Nope! We're all good here."

I also met my new primary care doctor last week, Dr. Marino—who is actually a family doctor who specializes in infants, who can see Baby when he or she is born. That appointment was also a breeze.

Dr. Marino: "I reviewed your records. No active problems right now?"

Me: "Nope, all is well. Feeling great."

Dr. Marino: "Wonderful. So, tell me about your diet."

Me: "I'm a Registered Dietitian, so just please trust me it's healthy."

Dr. Marino: "Haha, okay. What about exercise?"

Me: "Six days a week. I'm a marathoner."

Dr. Marino: "Well then. I guess I will see you again when you bring in the infant."

Maybe it sounds like I'm gloating about my good health. But if you consider the problems I've had the past year, you can see why I'm so glad to have a clean bill of health right now. I'm not taking it for granted.

Week 19 was the exciting ultrasound at the OB clinic. It's remarkable how much the baby has changed in just eight weeks since the last one. As I watched the monitor, I also watched Eric's face as he was turned toward the screen. He was beaming.

Eric and I explained we didn't want to know the baby's sex yet, but we asked the technician to write it down on a card I brought. The card is being mailed, inside another envelope, to my best friend Emma, who lives in the city where I used to live. Emma is coming here in two and a half weeks for work and is throwing us a small gender reveal party then. The card with the baby's sex on it will be sent to a bakery, who will make either a blue or pink cake, hidden under all of its frosting until Eric and I slice it for the grand surprise.

We already have names picked out; we came up with them within only a week or two after we found out I was pregnant. We are keeping the name a secret until the baby is born. I think it will be fun to know whether it's a boy or a girl, so Eric and I can refer to it by its name at home.

The technician said the baby's long bones are growing at just the right size, and everything looked healthy. She pointed out all of its major organs, commenting several times on how beautiful the heart's four chambers were.

"I'm glad to hear that," I told her. "Because I'm going in for a fetal echo in two days."

"What was the concern for the heart?" she asked.

The baby has to have a fetal echocardiogram because it was, though briefly and though not in its critical time of heart formation, exposed to lithium. The lithium that I started at Springview, after my negative pregnancy test. The lithium that I requested to taper off of, after my positive pregnancy test.

The cardiologist performing the echo was very kind. She reiterated what I already knew—that lithium has been associated with around a tenth of one percent risk of a heart defect called Ebstein's anomaly, and that taking the drug during the end of the first trimester could incur the risk. However, the cardiologist also said that the data is becoming more convincing that lithium's association with Ebstein's may actually be inaccurate; according to her, there may not truly be any risk at all.

I'd already stopped lithium before the window of risk—actual or not, so I haven't at all been concerned that my baby could have Ebstein's. I was so protective about risks that I insisted on tapering off lithium right away, even before I was on a therapeutic dose of Lamictal, which was only an accepted option because I was seeing both Dr. C and Holly every week for monitoring.

Why then, ever since the scheduling of the echo appointment, and climaxing in the waiting room for it, have I felt like I've done something wrong? Why have I felt like a careless and negligent mother? Why was I so ashamed, watching the monitor and the doctor capturing images on it, carefully typing in her findings?

Drugs have risks. They vary in frequency, they vary in severity. Obviously, minimizing risks and maximizing benefits is the goal, but the determination of where the risks outweigh the benefits is a very personal one.

Some of the medications used in bipolar disorder carry risks in pregnancy and breastfeeding. But what about the risks of *not* being on the medication? What about the importance of the increased risk of an episode without it?

Something that complicates this decision in bipolar disorder is that, while some drugs are safer in pregnancy than others, not all drugs are equally effective in different individuals. Finding the right drug—and more commonly plural—can take some discouraging trials of different prescriptions, doses, and combination treatments. So simply substituting one medication for another during pregnancy may not always be the most effective option, or the safest. It's challenging, and I'm sure these are very difficult decisions for physicians and their patients to make.

After I wiped off the ultrasound jelly from my belly and sat up, the cardiologist explained how everything looked perfectly normal with my baby's heart.

In Week 20, it finally happened. I knew it would, but it surprised me nonetheless: I couldn't zip my pants. While my weight gain has been pretty steady, my belly seems to have significantly protruded almost overnight. The main reason isn't because the baby is so rapidly growing—though it indeed is, now ten inches long and weighing in at over ten ounces. At this point in pregnancy, the uterus, which has remained low and nicely tucked down in the pelvic region, expands up in the abdomen closer to the navel; hence, my baby bump. I look pregnant.

Not only am I beginning to look pregnant, I'm also starting to feel pregnant. In fact, I'm feeling the baby move inside me. At first I thought I might just have some gas, or maybe a muscle spasm. But apparently the tiny internal twitches I feel are the baby, moving all around with its tiny limbs.

I feel the baby most when I lie down to sleep. Which is also when I feel my anxiety the most. My insomnia has worsened. Maybe that's why I've been feeling pretty sluggish this week. The easiness of the day that I had just a couple weeks ago has faded. My mood has been a little low, too.

Holly and I have been troubleshooting my sleep problems. It seems like I've tried everything.

I know the basics of good sleep hygiene. I go to bed around the same time every night and get up around the same time too—allowing eight to nine hours of bedtime. I've always been pretty regimented with my sleep routine. You have to be, when as a rapidly growing teenager swim practice starts at five in the morning and you live over half an hour away. I'm lucky that this has long been established for me, because for many newly diagnosed bipolar patients, setting a habitual sleep pattern can be difficult to actually implement and can feel like a major lifestyle limitation. So the scheduling hasn't been hard for me; the actual falling and staying asleep has.

I know how to create the sleep environment. Cool room temperature but not cold. Comfortable bedding. A noise cancelling air purifier. Plus ear plugs. Loose, breathable, soft clothes to sleep in. The perfect pillow. And now for my changing body, a pillow between my knees. No lights whatsoever. All phones silenced. Quarantining my spouse, who fortunately is a

Bipolar and Pregnant

quiet sleeper, to the guest room when he's sick. A weighted blanket.

I know what to avoid to help ensure sleep. Excessive caffeine, and none after lunchtime. Alcohol. Working out or eating a large meal right before bed. Emotional conversations before bed. High-energy music, highly engaging TV or books, and—the sin of insomniac sins—the blue light of a screen.

I have ways to relax to prepare my body for sleep. Progressive muscle relaxation. Stretching routines. Yoga. Slow breathing. Chamomile tea. Hot baths. I've even gone so far as to have candlelit bubble baths. Wonderful as all these things feel, even if I fall asleep, I inevitably wake up in the wee hours of the morning, unable to fall back asleep.

I pray. I read biographies with my Kindle blue shade. I move to the couch. I pet my dog with my eyes closed. I visualize myself swimming laps, only hearing the underwater swooshes of the pool.

Lately, I cry.

Nothing works.

I saw Dr. C this week. He had spoken with Holly, who had relayed my worsening anxiety with him.

Dr. C is easy to talk to. He seems like an empathic physician. I sense he really does wish well for me.

Nevertheless, it's easier to be open with Holly. I'm sure that's natural—she's a therapist, and I spend far more time with her. She knows me so very well, and she has been a haven of unconditional warmth for me. Sometimes it's difficult, and sometimes it takes a while, but I can tell Holly anything. It's an outstanding level of safety I have with her, only surpassed by my relationship with Eric.

I know Dr. C doesn't judge me. I also remind myself that even at my worst, my psychiatric problems are probably just a dime a dozen in his professional daily schedule of patients. But still, I felt like I'd failed somehow, when I confirmed what Holly had told him—that my anxiety and insomnia were getting very bad. When you're "Type A", self-reliant, a people-pleaser, and someone who still struggles with shame over mental health problems, it's sometimes impossible to be able to talk about problems without minimizing them.

I could tell you what the carpet of every psychiatrist I've ever seen looks like, I've looked down at them so much while talking.

Dr. C said he thought an SSRI would help, and I agreed. Over the past nine years on and off one, I believe I've always done better with anxiety while taking it. He explained it was safest to initiate the drug—the same one I'd taken for years without problems—at a low dose and increase it slowly.

You might think that, with my history of severe depressions, taking an anti-depressant would be a given. However, unlike their success rates with recurrent unipolar depression, they're not always helpful maintenance medication in bipolar disorder. In fact, they can even be harmful.

Anti-depressants can trigger mania in bipolar patients, but from what I've read, I'm at lower risk for this happening. The switch to mania with anti-depressants happens more often in bipolar I patients, and especially patients who switch between poles frequently and quickly; I have never experienced full mania, and all of my episodes have had months of stable mental health between them. Further, I have stopped and started this SSRI a

Bipolar and Pregnant

few times without any side effects or mood switches. An SSRI might be safe and helpful for me.

Dr. C scheduled our next appointment for the following week, and I agreed to call him if I noticed any symptoms of hypomania emerging. I'm so tired I can hardly remember what those felt like.

I have had three friends the past two weeks confide in me that they just found out they were pregnant. The third was Dani.

Dani was pregnant before. Just before we met at Springview. She had a miscarriage, and depression ensued. She's worried about it happening again, she told me. She wants to feel excited, but she's had her hopes crash before.

Miscarriage is on my other two friends' minds too. They're keeping their pregnancy secret until their second trimester. They're worried about what they eat, about exercising safely, and, ironically, they're worried about whether stress can cause a miscarriage.

I didn't hold any of these fears. For some reason, I was able to leave it to God to keep the baby alive in my womb. Why I worry about some things and not others doesn't make sense. Pregnancy is probably the time I'll worry the very least about my present motherhood.

It's what happens after the next 20 weeks that I'm afraid of.

Chapter 6. Weeks 21-24

Thirty-seven to one.

That's the ratio in Bipolar II of time spent in depression to hypomania, I've read. Nearly *forty* times as long.

This chapter opens with Week 21 of pregnancy, but I'm writing this several weeks after 21. Back in Week 21, whatever I wrote felt forced. It was a little jumbled, and it all had the harsh start-and-stop sentence structure and junction of ideas that a fourth grader might use in writing a story.

In Week 22, I raised a white flag to Writer's Block and stopped trying.

By Week 23, I was certain this whole project was a complete waste and was dumbfounded that I'd ever started it.

And in Week 24, I thought that, far beyond the uselessness of this book, my own life itself was meaningless.

Depression. It always takes me by surprise. Even knowing it'll be a recurring condition with bipolar disorder, even knowing all its warning signs, I still feel taken aback and completely fooled — downright violated — whenever I recognize it has taken up domicile within me. I knew it would come back for me to fight; yet the truth is, it feels unbelievable that it struck. Again.

In writing a book on bipolar disorder, I knew I'd need to write about what depression is like. But, as I was humming along so smoothly, I fully assumed I would tell you about my most recent, fully past and finished, episode of D5. That episode was so long and dark and deep that I figured whenever I hit a lull in my journal, I could rely on this past account and explain the dreadfulness of bipolar depression just fine without re-experiencing it in pregnancy.

The statistics alone warned I was at risk. I've read that about 70 percent of pregnant women with bipolar disorder experience a mood episode—predominately depression—during their pregnancy. Research shows that pregnancy does not protect against mood episodes, so my having a pattern of suffering my past 3 depression episodes each less than a year between the other suggested a likelihood of recurrence during my pregnancy.

My pregnancy opened in a hypomanic episode, and maybe the creative juices that surged with it, though much diluted after my short Springview stabilization, conceived the ideas for starting this book. Most assuredly, if it had opened in a depression episode, I'd never have written this.

My mind *shrinks* in depression. At first, like the slight nearsightedness of my blue eyes, things in the distance appear blurry; my field of vision becomes smaller. Then, as it closes in further, what appeared to have been blurry perception morphs into actual opacity, separating me from the rest of the world. Separating me from expanse of thought, expanse of desire, expanse of hope. It all closes in.

Writer's Block hinted at depression, but the apathy towards writing—yet another hint gone unnoticed—kept me from seeing the clue.

I saw Dr. C in Week 21. Between this appointment and the previous one, a lot had changed to make me very concerned for my mental health. And it all started with a cold.

And that's how easily it can start. A night of back pain, or maybe an upset stomach. A night of taking care of a sick child.

It can start with a deadline rapidly approaching. All it can take is some stressful conflict, or some kind of relationship crisis. Or it can start with a fun night that bleeds into morning, when you're young and wild and free or something like that.

It can start with travel—heaven knows it can start with jumping time zones, especially on red-eye flights for someone who can't sleep on planes.

A night without sleep. The number one trigger of a manic episode. The Most Feared event I have of setting myself off on a train wreck with a 100mph collision.

For me, it started with a cold. Who can ever make it through a winter without one? Eric and I both started getting it over the weekend, though he took the bigger hit. He had only been sick once in our marriage, and he's not one of those men who turn into helpless babies at the slightest sniffle. But I'm quite a natural at the mothering role to a sick husband, and he let me take care of him. I bought us the cold medicine and tissues, took Eric's temperature, refreshed his hot tea, and kept the dogs quiet and away from the guest room while he napped.

I was coughing, sneezing, and blowing my nose all day, but I didn't feel so awful. It was just a cold, and in a couple days, it would be over. With my never-ending doctor visits for my mental health, you might be surprised to know that I actually don't think you need to rush to the doctor every time you get a sore throat and sinus congestion.

In my favorite rotation of my clinical internship, I got to work with some leading GI doctors who were researching various aspects of the intestinal microbiome. With Crohn's disease, my

Bipolar and Pregnant

gut microflora might be attenuating or exacerbating my mucosal inflammation; the microbiome is a very complex organ of microorganisms.

One of the fastest ways to cause a seismic shift in someone's microbial colonies is to prescribe them antibiotics. The healthy order—the variety and quantity of different species—can be swiftly obliterated, causing damages scientists are only beginning to study. Antibiotics can be life-savers, for sure, but they're not as benign to the human body as they may seem.

Not to mention the fact that antibiotic resistance is now one of the top global health threats due to over-prescription. I read that the average American has already had seventeen courses of antibiotics by his twentieth birthday, many of which are very much unnecessary.

In college, the athletic department had a general practitioner come to campus in the evenings for us athletes to see if we became sick. His name was "Dr. Z". Well, that wasn't his name, but—no pseudonym here—it actually was his secret nickname among us athletes. We referred to him as Dr. Z because he was known to treat every physical ailment with a Z-Pak of antibiotics. Headache? Here's a Z-Pak. Strained hamstring? Take a Z-Pak.

I know this well-respected doctor wasn't just being lazy. Being the Not A Doctor that I am, I don't know for certain why he was so fast to throw broad-spectrum antibiotics at every symptom of a cold, but maybe, if you're treating a Heisman quarterback, you want to err on the liberal side of treatment. It wouldn't be good for your career, I am guessing, if the Olympic phenom you saw wound up getting a nasty infection and missing the most critical meet of the season with it.

And maybe that's how over-prescription of antibiotics occurs. Maybe everyone thinks they're some superstar, deserving of immediate treatment with the big guns.

So when I called Dr. Marino's office and requested an appointment for a "persistent cough", I felt fully compelled to state, "I know it's just a cough—No Big Deal. But I'm just concerned because it is keeping me up all night and I can't sleep."

Remember Dr. Marino? My new family doctor I just saw three weeks ago, as The Patient Who Is The Proud Epitome Of Health? Well the disappointment I had of returning Not Perfectly Healthy—and so soon—fit right in line with the low mood that was pervading my being.

A nurse brought me back to an exam room.

"If you have a cough, you need to wear this," she said, handing me a medical face mask. "I'll be right back to get your vitals."

She left the room, and I slipped the mask on, covering my nose and mouth. But after only a few moments, my anxiety soared.

I couldn't breathe. Lifting the mask, I tried gulping in air.

None seemed to enter.

I was panicking.

The periphery of my vision was black. I was going to suffocate without air, and my heart was going to explode.

As I closed my eyes, instantly filled with tears, oxygen finally entered my lungs, and I most gratefully exhaled. A few more panicky breaths, and tears streamed down my face.

Bipolar and Pregnant

The nurse re-entered. Immediately concerned, she asked me what the matter was, as I was shaking and trying to wipe the floodgate of tears, but they were dropping too fast. I whimpered something about having an anxiety problem and something about the face mask. Thankfully, I calmed down enough for her to get my vitals, and she left, telling me the doctor would be in shortly.

I wiped my eyes and took slow breaths. "I'm okay," I told myself. "I'm okay."

The friendly doctor entered the room, asking the preliminary questions about what brought me in. Obviously recognizing I'd been crying, he asked if I was all right, and I just told him I was fine—just sleep deprived.

He listened to my lungs, commenting on how they weren't entirely clear, but all I could focus on was breathing slow and steady, my hand on my stomach to be sure I was meeting this goal with a tangible rise and fall. Like I've told you, I hate being touched, and there's something extra vulnerable about a stethoscope and the requirement to relax and take slow breaths for a simple heart and lung check that gives me anxiety.

I told the doctor I'd have just let the cold pass—that I wasn't concerned about it and wouldn't have come in for just a cold. But I said, with all the dignity I could muster, that sleep deprivation was a serious matter for me because it could trigger manic episodes in bipolar disorder.

Dr. Marino nodded his understanding and said he thought a cough syrup with codeine—a powerful cough suppressant that also, as a narcotic, enhances drowsiness—would likely be quite helpful. Since he thought I'd only need it a few nights, he wasn't concerned about taking the small dose in pregnancy.

Part of me was thinking optimistic thoughts; it sounded like a good plan was in place. But, mostly, I was still on high alert, on the verge of tears and panicking, using every last drop of willpower I had to keep another attack from happening.

So when the nurse abruptly opened the door on us, I cracked. Flinching in one huge gasp, the walls closed in on me. The nurse and doctor apparently had some verbal exchange, she left, and, again, I was fast at work with damage control trying to mop my tears, but I couldn't keep up.

I don't remember what I said to Dr. Marino. Something about PTSD. Something about how I just needed sleep. Something about how I was usually Totally Fine and I was going to be Totally Fine and, please, no worries, ha-look-how-silly-this-is. I yanked myself together, smiled, and took the prescription he handed me.

I made it out to my car in one piece. And then I was free to let it all fall apart.

I couldn't do this. Everything was too overwhelming. Look what becomes of me after only one night without sleep!

I couldn't be a mother. And now my baby's pediatrician knew it too.

I slept five hours that night, my cough much better. But the next night, despite hardly coughing, I only slept three.

Since I'd gone these consecutive nights with very little sleep, I emailed Dr. C, telling him I didn't need cough medicine anymore but was very concerned for my sleep. He advised me to take a small dose of something I'd taken before for hypomania. I took it that night, and I slept a great eight point five hours.

Bipolar and Pregnant

The problem was, I felt drugged All Day Long. Being the trooper I am, I dragged myself to the gym according to my Daily Plan, and got on the treadmill.

But I couldn't run. In fact, I couldn't even walk. I was due to have lunch with my husband in about an hour and then see a matinee with someone, and all I could think about was how, if I got off the treadmill, I could go get in the back seat of my car, set my alarm, and sleep until lunchtime.

I met Eric in the parking lot of the restaurant. He asked how I was feeling, and I told him I still felt very drugged. As we were walking up to the front doors, I was mentally strategizing how I would get through an hour sitting without my face just dropping to the table. I balked at the tremendous undertaking lunch was going to be.

"Eric?" I said, stopping, standing still on the sidewalk. "I can't make it through lunch. I'm too tired. I need to go home."

He took me home, and I cancelled my movie plans. I slept hard for three hours and did Hardly Anything, at home, before it was bedtime again.

I decided to split the [already small] dose of medicine in half that night. Maybe it had hit me so hard because I was simply catching up on the sleep deficit.

But the next day, I felt drugged again—not quite as drugged as the previous day, but too tired to do anything more than Hardly Anything, again. What really made an impression on me was the recognition that I was still somehow full of energy at Springview when I started taking this drug—and at a dose a good five times bigger. Unquestionably, there was something biologically very wrong with my body in that hypomanic episode. Now, definitely *not* hypomanic, just a little of that medication knocks me out. So for the next couple nights, I opted instead for Benadryl, slept rather poorly, but at least was able to function in the day.

So you can see how anxiety and insomnia were my pressing concerns when I saw Dr. C in Week 21.

"I'm falling asleep okay," I explained. "I just keep waking up and can't stay asleep."

He explained his med recommendation for sleep, and then said we could increase the baby dose of SSRI I had started.

"It may take a couple weeks to be noticeable, but this may help with anxiety," he said. "And it should help with your depression too."

Depression? Who said anything about depression?

"I'm *not* depressed," I said, emphatically, leaning forward half a foot at least on the couch. "I always have suicidal thoughts when I'm depressed, and I'm not having any suicidal thoughts."

As I said, I'm writing this chapter weeks after this actual conversation took place. I remember it because of the strong defensiveness I felt.

'I didn't fail again!' I wanted to say. 'I've been doing all the Right Things! Surely I'm not guilty of this—you have to believe me!'

I simply couldn't be depressed again. Depression is neglecting to use all those skills I've been taught. Depression is a moral, spiritual failing.

Right?

While I'd already recognized my mood had been low, I insisted I wasn't depressed because I wasn't suicidal. Now that I have hindsight and some perspective, I can see the oversimplification I had in my criteria for depression.

Dr. C said something about degrees of severity in depression, along with signs and symptoms of depression aside from suicidal thoughts that still signify depression.

I think that deep down, I knew he was right. I think that deep down, I kept up my insistence that my mood hadn't reached depression because I was afraid of how bad things get When Depression Gets Worse.

But my mood had indeed changed. In Week 22, my best friend Emma came into town for a work-related event. She stayed with us the few days she was here, and she threw us a small party at a restaurant where we found out the sex of the baby.

Couples spend a lot of time excitedly wondering the sex of their baby. Sometimes they have hopes, but I imagine a preference is less pronounced with a first child than with subsequent ones. Eric and I had no preference. We just hope for a healthy one.

Because Emma's flight arrived just before the party, I was responsible for picking up the cake she ordered, which hid either pink or blue frosting inside to reveal whether the baby is a girl or boy. I felt like I should have been more impatient with enthusiasm to find out what was inside. But instead, I was thinking about the whole burden of entertaining Emma several days and of facing a couple dozen people that evening at the party—all the effort that engaging in conversation takes with depression.

It didn't help matters that the bakery I suggested for Emma took me through the same town as Springview. Just being over there gives me a pit in my gut. Cat has taken me on several runs through there, and each time, I've borne a somber spirit, cloaked in a resigned sadness.

Remember that half marathon I ran, the weekend after I left Springview, the morning after I found out I was pregnant? The course took us right through Springview's neighborhood. With all my fears when I saw those two lines on the pregnancy test, with all my worries about what was to come that morning before I told Eric, imagine how I felt running through the neighborhood where I'd been contained, assigning to others the responsibility of something I could no longer handle—keeping myself from killing myself? Imagine what it felt like to pass through there, less than one week from trading my hospital bracelet for the race bib I was running in, knowing not only how daunting it would be to keep myself on this side of life and wellbeing, but that the safekeeping of a baby lay inside me then too?

I thought that maybe several exposures to the area while mentally doing well would decondition my negative thoughts about the neighborhood, and I thought picking up the cake wouldn't bother me. But it did, and it probably always will.

There are reminders of the hells of depressions everywhere.

Thankfully, walking into the restaurant with Eric and Emma and a colossal cake in tow, my anxiety was low enough to be largely ignored. Our guests were having a great time over dinner, and I was getting excited for the cake to be brought out.

When it was finally time for the cutting, I put my hand over Eric's, wrapped tightly on the handle of the long knife. We looked into each other's eyes, right into each other's hearts, and I was instantly awash with emotion for the father of our child, with the same love I had nearly two years ago as we cut our wedding cake, with our friends and family there as celebrating witnesses. The same committed love, now with a new dimension of tenderness and trust.

As Eric cut into the cake, I cheered. It didn't matter what color was inside. I had a life partner to be there with me for this child.

The frosting was pink. We are having a girl. Our baby daughter is inside of me.

Having Emma around that week did me a lot of good. It kept me distracted. It even kept me entertained; she is, after all, my best friend. She gave me someone to think about other than me, and with Emma there, I could not simply collapse and hide in bed all day.

Depression is obsessed with itself. It's a masochistic illness that, without intervention, propels itself into greater harm with each passing day, like a cancer of the mind. Depression expresses all those lovely interleukin-6 behaviors of reduced activity, diminished motivation, and that profoundly compelling desire to allow malaise to just claim its victory already.

Somewhere along the way, some genius coined the term "behavioral activation", part of a dual intervention to combat depression alongside changing one's thinking patterns, and—behold—the manualized, researchable treatment of cognitive behavior therapy, dubbed CBT, was born. All Us Therapized Depression Survivors have undoubtedly been exposed to CBT's tenet of behavioral activation, wherein changing your behaviors can effectively change your emotions.

Behavioral activation and I are BFF's. As you know, I'm a disciplined lover of routine, and having a checklist of behaviors to engage in and a daily schedule to keep while depressed only becomes difficult when my depression has reached a Very Severe level.

For example, the two weekday evenings I attempted suicide, I'd gone to work that day. My second attempt, I came home directly from a fall pumpkin-carving party in my neighbor's backyard — an engagement I kept, not ever having come close to learning of CBT, because I instinctively knew that keeping up with Normal Life might just help me keep from Completely Falling Apart.

However, I'd found weekends to be nearly impossible, back then. I had nowhere I was expected to be except church Sunday and didn't really know how to set up a system of getting out and about and keeping myself out of bed those eternally horrible two days. So, now that I'm not working, I'm in a similar bind.

However, I'm now much better at making structure that forces me out, even when I don't have to report somewhere like an office. Plus, with my thinking so slow in depression, I'm afraid I'd not be able to keep up or would have more panic attacks if I were working and would need to take time off anyway. I think I'd be so uncomfortably overwhelmed; after all, I did come home after work and break down right into those two suicide attempts. Maybe it's good right now that I'm not trying to juggle so much. For now, I'm handling what I can handle.

It is now Week 23, and the baby weighs a pound and is about the size of a mango. I feel it — I mean HER — moving a lot more now.

It's a little strange saying "she" and "her" and hearing Eric call her by her name. Maybe because it addresses the reality that eventually I'll have a real human baby girl to take care of, and it's so much easier not to face this fear right now.

This week Eric took me out to see a movie, followed by dinner at an elegant restaurant in a hotel. I'd just bought my first maternity shirts, and this was my first outing in one. I'd been getting by on my loosest and longest-fitting tops and sweatshirts, and I'd probably been wearing more of Eric's clothes than my own. But, with a scheme all its own, my belly was continuing to grow, and I was running clean out of options for feminine appearance. I'd staved it off as long as I could, but by Week 23, I'd simply needed some clothes designed for the new shape I was filling.

We passed a swanky bar on the way to our table, where other couples our age were standing with cocktails together—young, hip, and enjoying life as DINK's, the affectionate term my mom friends use for couples with Dual Incomes and No Kids. Eric beat the maître d' to seating me, and I took the ambiance in.

Everything is going to change. When we have the baby. The places we go, the things we do, and what we spend our time talking about. Everything is all soon going to dramatically change.

Sparkling water was brought to the table, and I placed my napkin in my lap. Beneath my growing belly, now accentuated with the new black blouse with white flowers I was wearing, a bow tied below my chest, like a perfectly wrapped package.

I looked to my hands in my lap, on the white napkin; my nails simply manicured, with a single coat of clear glossy polish; my skin a bit dry, weathering through this last night of winter; my band of diamonds on my left ring finger, half a size too big, just how it felt best. My hands.

These hands would hold hers. Her chubby little fingers, already practicing grasping right then, inside of me. Her delicate, intricate hands.

How could I have been entrusted with something so precious?

I looked to Eric. He was glad to have surprised me with this restaurant. I love it when he plans romantic occasions and pretends he came up with the idea out of the blue.

As I've mentioned, I had some cold feet when Eric and I were engaged, several months before our wedding. Well-meaning, sweet friends would ask me, all gooey, "Oh I bet you just can't imagine living life without him, huh!" The problem was, I could. Of course I could—I'd lived through the first thirty years of my life without him, and I'd never yet lived *with* him. So the safe bet was obviously that I could live without Eric. The real question became, would it be better to live life without him?

I loved Eric, and I thought he was a wonderful man. But ultimately, I chose to marry Eric because of the faith-based beliefs I have, that living life with Eric would give us more opportunity to experience and enjoy the unconditional love we reverberate from God. I married Eric to experience the special intimacy a husband and wife share—a life full of risks and hurts and disappointments...but with a shared union with God to give us the light to give love and forgiveness and grace to each other.

I have some great feminist friends who would pull their hair out in hearing me say this, but it's the truth: Eric completes me. And somehow, some-unfathomable-how, I complete Eric. Wait, hold on, let me explain! No, he doesn't fill some void in my heart (though he does fill it with joy), and he doesn't cover over all my insecurities (though if you've read this far, you know he does give me a tremendous amount of confidence and assurance). Eric completes me by living life with me, with all its nitty-gritty details, and showing me that, in spite of my faults, my insecurities, and my self-centeredness, I am already and irreversibly perfectly complete in the eyes of God.

Bipolar and Pregnant

This man, just a mere mortal like me, shares a profound union with me. Together, our sum is greater than our parts. And now, we have made a baby together.

Week 24 came, and with it an unsurpassed number of tears. Seemingly wholly indifferent—and truthfully, with bipolar disorder, it really is mostly indifferent—to my efforts, my depression was worsening. I was crying at the drop of a hat, and I longed to reside under a big dark quilt until the sun of a new season rose. My anxiety, too, was very bad.

I had an appointment scheduled with Dr. C. This time, I made up my mind to clearly communicate the extent of my depression and anxiety—the adrenaline in my body and my insomnia in the morning, and also of my fears of the future as a bipolar mother. Since my mind was so sluggish that I could hardly keep up with the simplest of conjunctions and transitions in the sentences and paragraphs of Everyday Verbal Communication, I decided the best way to let my psychiatrist know how my mental health was doing was to write it out.

As I've said many times, talking with a mental healthcare provider is difficult. It feels so very vulnerable to let anyone know that your mood and thinking aren't Within Normal Limits. With loathsome self-regard being itself a symptom of depression, my attempt at hiding my shameful symptoms only prevents my doctor from most effectively treating me.

What enabled me to write out the painful symptoms I'd been experiencing was something Dr. C had said in a previous appointment with him a few weeks ago that reinforced that I wasn't just a Medical Record Number to Dr. C.

Like myself, Dr. C is athletic. He competes in a sport I've never been involved with, but he told me he had been doing some cross-training in the pool. Knowing I'd been a swimmer, Dr. C asked me for advice on choosing a new pair of goggles.

He simply asked me for a recommendation on swim goggles.

It was so small, but it was powerful enough to bridge the chasm I'd imagined.

This week Eric and I have been talking more about our worries. Parents-to-be almost always have them. It's not just me but Eric too is going to be responsible for a helpless little person, and I understand from therapy, mostly through my discussions with Lindsay, how the home life plays a big role in who you'll become as an adult. The formative years we'll have with Baby are so important, and the weight of the accountability produces so much apprehension. Sometimes these fears intensify and mix with a certainty of failure, and my gut contorts and constricts till I feel like squeezing myself into a ball and trying to think of something else to stamp out the dread.

I'm not the only one with apprehension because Eric has some too, and for some reason that relieves me. Eric told me sometimes he thinks of Baby and worries about not pursuing the right track in his career. He worries about being the family provider, which surprised me when he told me, because he doesn't seem to ever worry, like I do.

Eric has been thinking about moving positions—a change that would alter his career path and also physically move us to another state. The decision is beginning to weigh heavily on his mind, and, in placing myself in his shoes, it must be stressful to be the sole provider for the family.

To worry about family finances has never crossed my radar in pregnancy. Eric has a good job history, and even more, he has made many smart investments, in real estate and other funds that I, being quite risk averse, could have never managed. When we were married, he showed me with a detailed spreadsheet where all of our assets were and why they were there. I feel financially secure.

In fact, basically, I have always felt financially secure. I've been careful with my money since I started working, especially because my salary was never big. For someone who could worry about so many things, I am very grateful that money hasn't been one of them. I have always felt protected from financial crisis as a single woman because I believed that if something bad were to happen, my parents, sated with means, would help me. It was a safety net that gave me peace of mind.

Many people do not have this luxury. For so many families, financial concerns are a top stressor. And for so many with bipolar disorder or unipolar depression, finances are especially difficult. Keeping a job through repeated episodes—and even breakthrough episodes happen with treatment, as you can see—isn't always within their control.

Imagine if I'd been asked to step down from my university position without Eric in my life. Imagine if that happened without Eric, and I were pregnant.

I have good confidence in Eric and his financial plan. I think we live comfortably below our means. This isn't too hard because we are pretty frugal, in general. We economize, and we don't buy everything we want. This doesn't bother me; in fact, I'm wary of money and prefer not having too much.

There are reasons for this. Foremost, contentment is the best luxury on earth. I understand you can be content with little and content with great wealth, but I fear that having an overabundance tends to lead, ironically, to greater discontentment. Jesus talked more about money than almost anything else; he gave more than twice as much counsel on money than faith and prayer combined! What we do with our money is important, and there is nothing wrong with building up a great mass of wealth. But the love of money and the ever-increasing greed for money can be a big pitfall.

This obviously isn't only a Christian concept. Think of all the horrible financial scandals in our nation's recent history. People are willing to do disgusting immoral and unethical things stemming from discontentment with money. Slippery slope.

Another reason I try not to get caught up in possessions is because I've been to South Africa twice, to help with orphans with AIDS, and I've stayed in impoverished villages there. They have no plumbing, no electricity, and usually, not enough food. I've seen the squatter towns like Soweto, sprawled out far as you can see of "homes" built of adjoining scraps of tin.

Seeing Africa changed me. That doesn't mean I don't take for granted all that I, like most of us in America, have. In fact, only two weeks after I returned from South Africa the second time, when I vowed I'd never again take for granted the comparative riches I had, I stood in my big walk-in closet, flipping through a whole row of great clothes, saying to myself, "Agh, I have *nothing* to wear today!" Our materialistic culture makes it so easy to be ungrateful with abundance.

An extra basis for my efforts to have caution against pursuing more money comes from my childhood. I grew up in a very wealthy family. With two siblings and myself, a mom, and a dad, we had five beautiful BMW's parked at our six thousand square foot home. And inside that gorgeous house, the fighting was endless, and it seemed the ever-present conflict was about money; there was never "enough" money.

Bipolar and Pregnant

I'm grateful for our much less affluent lifestyle with Eric. If we can be wise with what we have and have hearts of thankfulness and a home that treasures love beyond anything, we will always be okay.

I know Eric shares this same view. We talked about these things a whole lot during our year-long engagement. Dissatisfaction with what we have hasn't taken a footing in his heart. I love this about him.

But I also know he wants to be the best dad he can be, and to him this means being able to provide means for Baby to excel in her pursuits. While I'm only able to focus week-by-week on taking care of the baby, by taking care of myself, Eric is such a long-term planner that he's already thinking about finances and the implications of some strategic career moves between now and when the baby is finished with college.

When I think about family finances, I can't help but think I'm a burden with my mental illness. We'd already chosen that I wouldn't seek employment, except maybe some side projects, throughout the rest of my pregnancy and probably until our baby went to preschool. However, I was asked to resign because of absences incurred while hospitalized with mental health crises. Whether you think it's fair or not, my university employer was bearing this burden.

People with bipolar disorder often need to take time off from work to handle acute illness. This is costly. I've read that the costs of major depression in the U.S. total a burden of over two hundred *billion* dollars a year, mostly through lost productivity. Depression is only surpassed by back injury in being the most costly medical condition in employment.

It's a disabling, financially onerous illness.

There are other costs as well. Medical bills—hospitalizations, psychiatry appointments, therapy appointments, all those necessary but loathed medications—even with good insurance coverage, these costs all add up to something Not Small.

Fortunately I've never engaged in extravagant spending in hypomanic episodes. The lost inhibition in mania is very commonly expressed in excessive spending. Remember my friend Callie with bipolar disorder? She went berserk shopping online in manic episodes. Her father's manic episodes drove the family into bankruptcy more than once.

Manic episodes can also incur financially costly legal problems. Reckless behaviors can cause damage to self, others, and property, and often this involves breaking the law. Driving recklessly, picking bar fights, abusing alcohol and other substances—behaviors that the manic person would not ever engage in while his or her Usual Self can have huge financial and other punitive costs.

Bipolar disorder is expensive. I am too, and, despite Eric's consistent reassurances to me, I feel guilty about this.

While it can be a relief knowing that Eric also has some of his own worries about raising our baby, truthfully inside, when I think about my own, his are a major affront to my self-assurance as a parent. My biggest concern is immeasurably different. My biggest fear is that my baby won't have a mother.

Because her mother killed herself.

Chapter 7. Weeks 25-28

Suicide.

Suicide is a most difficult subject. It's bleak. It's painful. It's disturbing.

But it's real.

I hate that there is so much stigma with suicide. I hate that Daniel's funeral didn't use the word, and that Jane's friends didn't know what to say after he died, so they simply said *nothing*. Dan as his Usual Self wouldn't have ended his life. Bipolar disorder killed Daniel.

Bipolar disorder is a potentially fatal illness. Are there better ways doctors can talk about these risks with patients so that we don't have to feel so ashamed about suicidal thoughts before they're overwhelming? Instead of asking whether we're having suicidal thoughts with an expectation of a dichotomous yes or no answer, can "maybe" be incorporated into the dialogue? Are there better ways to talk about suicide, to open the Door to Help that a patient would otherwise shut out of shame?

Suicide is the cause of death in approximately 15% of those with bipolar disorder. One out of seven of *us*. I'm in this pool. Which side of the 15% will I end up being on?

I don't think you can ask yourself that question and have uncertainty in your answer, like I do, unless you've ever anguished with suicidal thoughts or have attempted suicide. If you've never been entombed in this darkness, I don't think you can truly understand what it feels like.

But I'll do my best to show you.

Time is a farce. Minutes, days, weeks—time is not a measurable unit but the essence of hell. A moving clock is a testimony to the devastating reality that I'm still here, and if I think about how the hands flow around the center without pause and without an end, my heart pounds and my throat closes desperately tight.

Suicide is *impatient*. Even knowing my body will eventually die, without any intervention towards that end on my part, suicidal thoughts beg me to hasten an end. I cannot wait for nature to take its course.

The pain has to end, and it has to end soon.

None of my depressions have lasted forever. And I don't believe any future episodes won't eventually subside. But when depression reaches the severity of suicidal thinking, not only does enduring the present episode seem impossible, but, especially, the thought of future episodes recurring in my life easily convinces me that life is not worth living.

When I have suicidal depression, I see methods and means to end my life everywhere. Dangerous as well as ordinarily innocuous objects are ubiquitous, thrusting themselves to the forefront of my vision as potential portals to end my hopeless pain. Bridges, trucks, ropes, knives, exhaust pipes, cyanide, and pills—so many pills.

In D5 it was trains. I thought of jumping in front of a train ten thousand times. I imagined the dim underground station, the noise of the vehicle to peace as it sped on its tracks towards me, the last leap I'd ever make.

Bipolar and Pregnant

Just one simple—utterly simple—leap. And it would all be over.

I can tell you what my two suicide attempts, eight years ago, felt like: Nothing. The first time, I opened my medicine cabinet, and instead of taking one pill of prescribed antidepressant, I poured the rest of the plastic rusty-colored pharmacy bottle into my hand and swallowed as many as I had left. The other medicine in my cabinet was Tylenol, so I must have figured I'd swallow whatever remained in it, which was close to the whole bottle of 50 pills.

I was hospitalized and returned home. But now that I was The Girl Who Attempted Suicide, who was obviously deranged and couldn't be trusted, my resolve to try to endure that D2 was even more depleted. Along with the boxes of cereal I was subsisting on, I replenished my Tylenol at the grocery store, this time opting for additional assurance by choosing a bottle of 100.

About three weeks later, I swallowed all 100. I don't remember deciding to do that. But I remember thinking about jumping in front of an 18-wheeler countless times. I lived near a busy freeway, and, with my window cracked, hearing sounds from the road was practically a lullaby each night, shushing my crying.

I think that there is a point of no return with suicidal thinking. I don't know where that point is, and I didn't notice when I had crossed it, back eight years ago. But last summer in D5, I knew without a doubt I was toeing the line. I sensed, with the last remnant of life within my veins, my hope was about to finally dry up. And then I'd be gone.

But I told somebody.

I know this sounds like a strange thing to say, but I saved my life in D5. It would have been the *easier* thing to do, to keep my suicidal despair inside and let it claim its victory, and, probably magnetically and without any true effort at all, leap in front of that train I'd thought of so many times. It would have been *easier* to let gravity keep pulling me forward and downward, over the line where Living is no longer an option. But I felt gravity's tug, and I resisted, with the vapor of Life in me that still remained.

Last June in D5, I was in Dr. C's office, and our appointment had just ended. We had scheduled our next appointment, and it was time for me to stand up and leave. But I didn't.

Instead, I told him. I don't remember any of my words. We've never since talked about it. But I know I must have told him how much I wanted to die and that it was soon going to be more than I wanted to live. That I couldn't go on. That I needed someone to help me keep myself from me.

Eric was out of town for work and got on the very next flight home, meeting me at an ER where a couple from my church had taken me after picking me up from Dr. C's office. I have no idea what I said to them, and I have no idea what time that night I was admitted to Springview. I don't remember most of the next month there either.

But I sincerely believe, if I'd have made it to Dr. C's door and had left, I wouldn't be here writing this.

I understand how Daniel left Jane. It's exactly how I was about to leave Eric.

Suicide is utter *aloneness*. I don't think it's "selfish" like some people label it. Actually, thoughts of relieving everyone of the burden I am fuel my suicidal wishes. Suicide is the final loss of connection, to the lives outside of you.

Can the feeling of connection tether me to this side of life? Can I keep working on building trust and love and intimacy in my relationships—living life richly, and maybe these ties will keep me from leaving? Can I maintain connection with God through daily conversation with him and through close relationships with other believers for encouragement in depressions?

The only explanation I have for why this current depression in the middle of my pregnancy hasn't plagued me with suicidal thoughts isn't just because I feel some connection to others outside of me, but because I know there is a precious life *inside* of me.

I saw Danielle in Week 25. It was a lovely day, so we decided I'd bring Lucky and she'd bring her little dog on a long walk together.

"How are you doing?" I asked her, as we set off down a shady path by a river I like to run alongside. My question wasn't a mere salutation; my tone expressed my concern for how she was holding up.

She had recently text messaged me her awful news: She had a miscarriage. Again.

Dani just sighed and shook her head. But she said she was doing better than last time. And she said she'd been taking different medications with the new psychiatrist, who I've heard is really great, she's seeing, and that she's feeling better and is hopeful for their protective effects against the postpartum-like depression she plummeted down into last time.

As we walked along, Lucky chasing after squirrels, I felt guilty. I wished I could suck my stomach in and not be a reminder of what she lost. It didn't seem fair that I was the one who was quietly having a hard time accepting that I was going to have a baby, while she was the one who longed and yearned for one.

Eric and I got pregnant within one cycle. I didn't use the help of a calendar or an iPhone app, or anything at all to strategize for best odds. I've read that, for our ages, by simply doing Business As Usual, only about one in seven couples see those two blue lines in one month; the average for our age is about five months.

Much as I was wishing I was average and that I could have had time to adjust to the changes I was experiencing as a newly unemployed bipolar patient, when I came home with Lucky that afternoon, pouring her some fresh water, and stretching out my slightly aching back, I was thankful for my fertility. I've been so caught up in the difficult timing of my conceiving that I haven't even thought about how blessed I am to be able to conceive at all.

Setting aside in my journal right now all the fears I currently have about my fitness for motherhood, I have always wanted to be a mother. Motherhood has been an important part of my dreams for my future — for the life I hope to live and the legacy I want to leave behind.

Eric too has wanted to be a father. We discussed these desires when we were dating, and we agreed that if we for any reason couldn't have children of our own, we'd want to become parents through adoption. Because I've always been perfectly normal and healthy with my reproductive indicators and doctor checkups, I'd assumed I wouldn't have any fertility trouble. Now, in thinking about the all-too-common sorrows of miscarriage and infertility, I can see how crushed I'd be if I kept trying to have a baby only to learn that I couldn't.

Bipolar and Pregnant

My mental health has been very rocky this week. The average mood has now fallen to a two out of ten. I feel panic attacks brewing. And I cry several times a day.

One of my worst sobfests came this evening. Sitting on a curb, in a parking lot. Pretty close to rock bottom.

Eric and I had taken a long walk together after he got off work, on the same bike path that Cat and I often ran on. I use the past tense, because a few weeks ago, Cat and I stopped running together.

"Cat," I said to her one evening on that same bike path, on what was for her a short recovery run and for me therefore a rather high-intensity one, "I'm going to have to say farewell to running with you after today."

Cat is training for the local marathon that a lot of our friends are running. She has put in a lot of hard work for the race, and I didn't want her to feel like she was abandoning me to run alone instead of with me on our regular duo workouts together.

"You see, you're only going to be running faster, and I'm only going to be getting slower."

"Aw," she replied. We were loping along at what was for her an easy pace, but for me one that already made me wonder if I could hold on the whole six miles with her.

"Well, what if you just run with me on my easy days?" she suggested.

I laughed. "It has already come to that. I can barely keep up, and I'm slower every day."

Cat made a playful pout face. "I'll miss you." And I knew she meant it. I'd miss our regular time together too. She's a dear friend and a very important person in my life. Sure, we can still see each other, but it's harder, with the busyness of life—hers especially. And it's not the same. Our friendship revolves around a 160 heart rate.

"Fly free, little birdie," I replied, and we finished what will be the last duo of ours for several months. After I've become a mom.

Eric and I got into an argument on our walk. Of all things, it was about a run stroller. I wanted him to come with me after our walk to pick it up. He thought he had a better idea, which to me wasn't a better idea, so, being the one who is always Quick On His Feet, complete with a career in the art of persuasion and negotiation—someone who probably should have been his high school's star champion of the Debate Team instead of their football quarterback, Eric swiftly began laying forth the first argument to support his claim.

I tried to keep up. I was able to respond with a decent counterargument, and then I awaited his reply.

My first degree was in Communication. One of my favorite courses was "Argument and Persuasion", and I used the few elective credits my degree permitted to take two "Logic and Reasoning" courses in the Philosophy department of my university. I enjoyed writing sound, beautifully threaded, thesis-driven papers. Many times, the arguments I used in my papers were formed in my head during swim practice. There was something about impelling my cardiovascular system to enliven my muscles to move me forward with graceful speed in the water that also accorded my mind to bring forth ideas, bond the choice ones together, and—all in my swim-capped head—*write*.

Bipolar and Pregnant

For whatever reason, I am able to produce words vastly easier with pen and paper than with my voice. It probably has something to do with fear. Fear of missing the mark with my reasoning, fear of the other person's superior response, and, most likely, fear of what the other person sees in me.

It's easier to hide behind mere black letters on a white page.

Our first few months of marriage were challenging. We both avoided conflict, because usually when we engaged in it, it didn't go well. We have learned so much, and now we are able to grow in our relationship with one another *because of* conflict.

One important lesson we learned about ourselves in engaging in healthy conflict came during an argument after work at our old apartment. We lived across the hall from Cat. (We actually met at run club and then came to find out we were living mere feet away from one another!) Eric and I had been making our cases, back and forth, and I was only millimeters away from either Totally Shutting Down or, in the same frustration, saying something Very Unkind. Fortunately this time, before I could make a turn for the worse, Caitlynn rang the doorbell. We'd agreed to go for a run together that night, and there she was, laced up and ready to hit the city streets with me.

"We have to pause this," I sighed to Eric. "I'll be back in an hour."

Cat and I did our run, talked about who knows what, and I came back home. I slid off my shoes, poured a big glass of water, and sat down next to Eric at his computer.

"How was the run?" he asked.

"Great. Hey, why don't we pick up where we left off? I'm ready now, if you are."

"Sure," he said, sliding his laptop away and facing me.

"And, Eric? I think I needed that whole hour to become ready again."

I remember this argument because of how at Just The Right Moment, right before it was Too Much for me to handle, the doorbell rang, giving me the break that I needed.

My endurance isn't the same as Eric's. I can become emotionally and cognitively flooded, and that's what happened tonight, walking back with Eric.

I stopped hearing whatever it was he was saying. I just started crying. And I couldn't stop.

"I'm so sorry," he said.

"You didn't say anything wrong," I told him. "I just have to take a break."

He led me to his car, but I couldn't even wait for him to unlock it. I just collapsed right there on the curb, for who knows who all to see, and poured out tears, my chest to my knees.

Whatever stamina I usually have, only a small fraction exists in depression.

Eric sat down next to me.

"I'm just so tired," I said, wiping at my completely wet face. The tears wouldn't stop. "I just can't keep going."

After a couple minutes there, Eric unlocked the car and we each got in. There was no use anymore in trying to stop crying. But as completely undone as I felt, I wasn't useless. There was something I was able to do.

Another argument that was a positive landmark in our marriage occurred in our bedroom, both of us sitting on the bed. The tension was rising; boy, I could feel it.

Without a gap in what we were saying, I stopped tugging on my hands, as I tend to do when I'm very anxious, and I placed my hand lightly on his arm. Just for a few seconds.

That argument never became a fight. Instead, it led into one of the most important discussions we've had. With touch, I told Eric I was on his side. With touch, he dropped his shield.

In the car, a total mess, I placed my hand on Eric's arm. We sat in silence a long while.

"Sometimes," Eric said slowly, "I get into discussions, at work, or with family, and I feel like I'm getting nowhere. It doesn't happen very often, but sometimes I feel myself approaching this breaking point, when I want throw my hands up and walk away. I get to where I feel so exhausted, and it would be so much easier to just give up."

I listen to my husband, my closest friend, my greatest ally.

"I can't imagine fighting that all throughout the day like you do in depression. Like you've been doing. Like you are doing right now."

New tears came. Tears of hope, tears of gratitude.

"You understand," is all I could say.

Katie McDowell

I saw Dr. Hillary Hanson, the perinatal psychiatrist, in Week 26, nearly five months since my initial appointment with her. As an expert in psychiatry with women's reproductive health, seeing Dr. Hanson would enable her to give Dr. C the best recommendations as a specialist for this unique time in my life. I'm always really appreciative when two doctors work together for me.

Dr. Hanson took an inventory of my symptoms: poor sleep, very low mood, feelings of hopelessness, fatigue, avoidance of people, and an arduous cognitive sluggishness. Plus anxiety rising up to the roof, having now had four separate full-blown panic attacks.

Dr. Hanson discussed some medication changes with me that she communicated would likely improve some of my symptoms quickly. As much as it bothers me to need medication, the thought of alleviating what I was enduring was compelling enough for me to stamp out any reluctance.

Depression is a painfully conflicted beast. While it seeks to engage in nothing but itself, it simultaneously begs for relief.

Medications have been able to provide tremendous relief for me, and I have been more accepting of the ones that show effects quickly—like benzodiazepines, and sleep aids like mirtazapine and zolpidem. Dr. Hanson conferred with Dr. C, and I dragged my miserable self to the pharmacy to pick up the new drugs.

That very night, I slept better than I had in weeks, and the next day, my anxiety was seriously cut in half. It's amazing how much I felt better, physically and mentally, so quickly; medications can be a big game-changer.

My beliefs about mental illness and the role of medication are rooted in my worldview as a Christian. These are issues I've struggled with, that I've been inconsistent with, but that ultimately can't be separated from my faith—which itself, as you've probably seen, isn't fully mature. But I can see evidences over time that my faith is growing, and the important topic of medications in bipolar disorder illustrates an area of growth.

Though I have said before that I don't believe spiritual problems cause my depressions, that wasn't entirely precise. Mental illness is a part of living in a broken world, where there are heartaches and, ultimately, death. Some of the problems we face are consequences of something we've done (our own spiritual antecedent); other times, they're consequences of the original sin of Adam and Eve, when they defied God and brought upon the human race and the world in which we live a curse. As members of the human race, we are, without faith, still seen as children of Adam and separated from God; however, with faith in Jesus whose holy life was a ransom and substitute, God doesn't go against his own holiness to accept us as his own children.

Though I believe, through my faith, I am a child of God, meanwhile, I still live in a broken world. A world with fatal car crashes. A world with cancer.

A world with mental illness.

I believe that bipolar disorder is not caused by a personal spiritual failing and that neither are the anxiety and PTSD that I suffer. I believe that, even in an imperfect world where these pains exist—and sometimes ravish in people, God gives temporal graces to show some of his attributes, like Comforter and Creator, and that a wonderful gift he gives me to enjoy is the discovery and development of medicine.

I can take the medicines that Dr. Hanson recommends and that Dr. C prescribes for me with a clear conscience. Yes, sometimes I'm inconsistent in my acceptance of these, and sometimes I as a person who is self-reliant to a fault feel shame for not being able to overcome bipolar disorder by willpower. But ultimately, I believe these drugs to be signs of compassion from a God who gives talents to some hard-working people to show them the science of a world he made, and I believe it's wise for me to accept drugs as compassion.

If you're not a Christian, this may all sound foreign and confusing and maybe even ridiculous. But my faith-based beliefs are core to my worldview, and to my story that makes up this book.

The mind and the brain are not one; neither are they distinct. Any patient who has learned some CBT knows this. My negative thoughts exacerbate my depression. My worries contribute to my physiological anxiety. How can I still have the Christian virtues of joy and hope and peace in the depths of depression and the agony of anxiety?

This is where the rubber meats the road. You've followed me through twenty-six weeks. Doubtless there are many things you've wished you could say to me that would help me or encourage me—ways where I've been my own worst enemy. Left to myself, I'd probably fall apart. But I do have people—not just Holly, who is uber-helpful—who show me where I can help myself with my mental illness, outside of taking medication.

Every week, I meet with two ladies from my church, Rita and Lily. Rita is a little younger than my mom, has basically lived in the same neighborhood her whole life, and is a chatterbox with a strong and fun personality. Lily is my age with a two-year-old son, is quiet, and always seems very content, and she shows a lot of genuine interest in others when she speaks. During our weekly meet-ups, either walking outside or drinking coffee in one of our homes, we purposefully share the deeper things that are happening in our lives.

Bipolar and Pregnant

Rita and Lily, therefore, have known about my bipolar disorder and my struggles with anxiety. They give me encouragement and support. This week's meeting, the same week as seeing Dr. Hanson and starting some new drugs, I told them about how I was working on my anxiety, simultaneously, from a spiritual side. I told them about the book I'd begun reading by a favorite Christian counselor on anxiety, fear, and worry.

"I have that book," Lily said. "I've read it four times!"

I shouldn't have been so surprised that Lily had read a book on this topic, because much of her encouragement to me has come through her own struggles and growth she has shared with us as we've talked. I thought of how good it is to have support like ours in a Christian community. Holly can help me see cognitive distortions; these women show me how to anchor my beliefs in our common hope of the gospel.

It didn't hit me until I left Lily's house that, not only had she needed to read a book on the same problem as me, but she has needed to read it *four* times! Lily, who seems to me so calm and carefree, fights the same battles I do. Over and over. Progress comes, but the problem will never fully be eradicated this side of Heaven. And so Lily persists in her effort, with the energy and freedom that come from knowing that God is honored by her efforts but already loves her unconditionally nonetheless. The goal isn't acceptance—I'm already accepted by God through my brotherhood with his son. The goal is a closer relationship; this is how faith grows.

Lily is an inspiration to me. I give up so easily. Faith is an endurance built up over time. The Bible tells of countless people who went through all sorts of hard circumstances and challenges, and through them their faith grew. Their understanding of God and the realization of their reliance on

God grew. God wants me to be close to him, so that I'll know his goodness.

Is this why he allowed me to have bipolar disorder?

A few days after seeing Rita and Lily, I got some gut-wrenching news: Lucky has cancer. I had noticed a small round bump on her skin near her armpit. I know dogs often get harmless cysts, but I wasn't sure about this bump, so I took her to the vet. After performing a needle aspiration of the lump, the vet came back into the room where my scared little Lucky and I were waiting.

"I looked at the aspiration under the microscope," the vet said, "and, though I'll send it to a pathologist for confirmation, I'm rather certain she has what is called a mast cell tumor, which is a malignancy."

She explained that it would need to be removed but that, if it was not an aggressive malignancy and if the tissue they removed around it didn't show malignant cells too, Lucky had a good prognosis of being cured with the surgery.

Those were a lot of "if's".

We scheduled the operation for the following week, and I tried my hardest not to think about it. Because every time I did, tears came to my eyes.

Oh, how I love my little Lucky.

A few days later, I ran an easy three-mile "shake-out" run with my run group, most of whom are running the local marathon this weekend. I was happy to see all of them together, and with my good luck wishes to them I received in return many cheery belly pats.

Bipolar and Pregnant

After our easy run, I walked to a nearby trendy coffee house where I'd planned to meet Eric, who had some work to do there while I'd read. On my walk, I wondered whether, if I weren't pregnant, I'd be running the local marathon this weekend too.

What else might I be doing if I weren't pregnant? How would these past 26 weeks have played out if I hadn't found myself on this life-changing path?

When I arrived at the coffee shop, I found Eric, who had beaten me there and had set up his laptop. He seemed to be already engrossed in his work, so I didn't say much, and I read quietly next to him.

Over the next hour, I'd said a few things to him, but he seemed quite distracted, till finally I assumed something was bothering him.

"Eric, is everything okay?"

He made a certain smile and nodded, which is his tell sign that not everything is okay.

"You just seem a little… Are you maybe in a bad mood?"

"No," he said, sighing. We have given each other full permission to be open about bad moods. "I just have some big problems with the work decision that I'm working out in my mind."

Eric's company wants to send him off to a different location and promote him. He has been offered a few different options—each in different states, and each with slightly different roles.

"Do you want to talk about them with me?" I asked.

"No, not yet," he said. He told me that his thoughts were a bit tangled and that he wasn't sure which choices made the best sense. He didn't want to overwhelm me, he said, but wanted to wait until he had nicely organized the options to present to me.

Eric doesn't have a science background and is at a loss when I chatter with my nutritionist friends. Likewise, I have never really understood exactly what Eric does for work. It does seem pretty complicated already, and if he tried to explain how the varying positions he's looking to fill are different from each other, I'd no doubt be confused.

Eric meant well. He knew I wouldn't understand, and, given my current cognitive crash in this depression, he knew I wasn't my Usual Self but would be quickly overwhelmed. He was trying to protect me from the stress he's been feeling about planning for his future in his career—plans that he knows also impact me.

But I felt left out. So I told him so.

"I know I probably can't help you make the strategic choice," I told him. "But it's something that's bothering you, and I want to hear about it from you. I'm sitting next to you, but we're a world away right now."

He understood, but he said, "I'm afraid discussing it would be premature, because I'm not very clear on the pros and cons myself."

"Babe. You don't need to solve this before telling me about it. At least we'll be in it together?"

I told him I was only repeating to him what he'd told me in my depression. That he usually doubted he could say anything helpful, but that he wanted me to tell him how I felt. Even if I didn't make much sense. Even if what did make sense was upsetting. He wanted me open, even when I was at my very darkest.

This is relational intimacy unlike I've ever before known. I just want to be beside him, as he wants to be beside me. I want to be there with him under the burden, because maybe, I can help him carry it too, in ways we can't foresee. I want in on his moody contemplation, and I want the opportunity to show him unconditional love when he broods. I want the depths of his frustrations, his weaknesses, and his dreams, all exposed, for me.

In Week 27, when I was—to my sheer delight—approximately 26.2 weeks pregnant, Cat and several other friends ran our local marathon (a marathon being 26.2 miles). It was a gorgeous day, and I brought Eric along with me to cheer. When most of my friends had passed our cheering post, Eric and I walked down the street for pizza.

As we strolled down the sidewalk, Eric elbowed me with a smile.

"Did you see that girl we passed looking at you? Her smile was huge," he asked.

"What? No. What do you mean?"

"Your belly. You mean you haven't noticed all the smiles you've been getting?"

I was wearing a tight shirt that didn't hide my growing baby bump. Another couple approached us, and as they were passing, sure enough, they smiled at my stomach. I hadn't even noticed this effect. All sorts of people were smiling—smiling at new life, soon to emerge and be a part of us all.

I also hadn't even noticed during that day that I wasn't feeling depressed—a realization that came to me at my run club's post-race party later that afternoon with Eric. After watching my very tired friends push their way through the course while we cheered, it was really fun for me to show Eric how happy they all were afterwards, wearing their finisher medals in the restaurant we'd reserved.

They talked about the ups, they commiserated about the downs. Most of them didn't reach the times they hoped for, but everyone finished, and through victories and disappointments, as a parallel to life, they didn't give up. And for this reason, they all welcomed my congratulations, with pride.

Milling around the bar with my club soda, I spotted a girl who was with one of my runner friends, and we smiled a hello to each other. Continuing on back to where Eric was standing, I turned to look over my shoulder.

"I swear I know that girl. Not from running, but..."

"That's Jaime," he said. "You know...from Summer Camp."

"Summer Camp" was what we'd nicknamed my month-long summer stay at Springview Hospital, during a time we also nicknamed "The Great Depression."

"Ah, Jaime!" I said. "I'd have never figured it out. Good memory."

Jaime was my social worker in the hospital. I saw her nearly every day. I think Eric only saw her twice, for family meetings. Maybe Eric does have a good memory to readily recall her, nine months after I discharged from The Great Depression; I, for sure, have an atrocious one for that month.

Bipolar and Pregnant

I wanted to tell her hi, so I did. Careful to allow her to easily keep her HIPAA obligations, I simply told her that I'd been doing well since Springview (and, comparatively, this was quite true) and that I (obviously) was pregnant. We exchanged cheery well-wishes, and I ventured on to another table of my comrades.

Later that night at home, wiping off the mascara from my eyes at the bathroom mirror, I realized something.

This is D6.

This is my sixth depression—an inexplicable sadness I've been fighting the past several weeks. A depression that, with the addition of the new medications Dr. Hanson recommended, was actually becoming tolerable; not only was it not getting worse, it was getting better.

Part of what makes depression so painful is its tenacity in inflicting rumination in its host. Rumination was an aptly chosen word to describe the tendency in depression to chew on pain and suffering, swallow it, only to again spit it back up to chew on it all over again. The same negative thoughts—even the same thoughts *about* those thoughts circulate over and over, seeking to gain more ground with each cycle, staking ever more claim in the mind until all else is crowded out but the misery that bears and is borne by not only physical pains but *thoughts*.

When I am depressed, I tend to think a great deal about just how very depressed I am. Any patient who has been Cognitive Behavior Therapized knows that challenging the accuracy of these thoughts, or behaviorally distracting oneself from these thoughts, can help in depression. Maybe it was in part the excitement of the marathon and being outside on a beautiful day with my husband that helped distract me, but I think mostly I hadn't been caught up in rumination all day because my depression is doubtlessly lifting.

Just as I hadn't noticed the smiles from the strangers, I hadn't noticed that I was distracted—even merrily distracted—all day, until I saw Jaime. In D5, nothing helped to keep me from my psychic misery. My sole distraction was sleep, and even that was elusive without medication. Seeing Jaime caused me to make the comparison of D5 to this current D6 and see the dramatic contrast in their severity.

Why did this depression not plummet like D5? Has the mood stabilizer I've been taking been protective—obviously not to fully prevent depression, but to pull back on the reigns enough to keep it from reaching the severity I've known in previous episodes? Has my knowledge of the life growing inside of me, which has kept me from ruminating on suicide, held the floodgates of severe depression at bay?

In Week 28, I had my first major physical health problem related to pregnancy. Two minor ones I've been working through are strictly exercise-related, so I haven't bothered mentioning them to Dr. Greenberg: Achilles tendonitis and symphysis pubis dysfunction. For the past several weeks, my Achilles have been very tight during my runs, and—it's an odd pregnancy symptom, I know—my pubic bone hurts afterward. Not only the added weight, but the relaxin hormone that shoots upward in pregnancy causes ligaments to stretch, and apparently my lower legs and the little ligament joining together my poor pubic bone are taking some strain. But, seriously, these are No Big Deal.

What *is* a big deal is abdominal pain in pregnancy—especially pain that has progressed over several hours, especially when you have Crohn's disease.

I have had so many small bowel obstructions that I can easily identify their onset. Most of my obstructions are partial ones, and even the full ones have always cleared up within 48 hours of

IV steroids. Thus, I've never needed surgery, which is great, because generally, disease returns again just as it had been before, and usually adhesions from surgery causes more disease complications which, again, usually require surgery. I think of it like the divorce rate in the U.S.: Over half of Crohn's patients eventually require surgery, and if you get one surgery, you're even more likely to have a second.

This time, the quality of my pain was similar to my usual presentation of obstruction, but the location was much higher than its typical spot in the right lower quadrant—a place very near my appendix and always a concern for ER physicians treating me.

I had one particularly bad Crohn's flare-up in grad school and went to the ER.

"This is where your pain always is with flare-ups?" the salt-and-pepper doctor asked, palpating the bloody hell out of my extremely sensitive gut.

"Yes," I grunted.

"You still have your appendix?" he asked, finally taking his hands off my abdomen that felt like it was going to burst.

"I do, but I'd bet you a million dollars this isn't my appendix but a small bowel obstruction."

The doctor grinned. "A million dollars eh? Well I'll get you into imaging and try to make you as comfortable as possible for now."

After I'd had a CT scan and more than one dose of heavy-hitter narcotics, the doc appeared by my gurney.

"Well, I have good news and bad news," he said. "The good news is you win a million dollars because you have a small bowel obstruction."

I nodded.

"The bad news is," he said, dropping his grin, "you have a small bowel obstruction."

So, at home that afternoon with the pain, which I thought might have been higher than usual with intestines shifting upward to make space for the uterus, that wasn't subsiding, I decided to call my OB's office—a number I had to look up online because I, even being an amateur quasi-hypochondriac, had made it through to the third trimester with so few OB concerns.

The nurse instructed me to go to the obstetrics floor of the medical center where I'll give birth, where a doctor could examine my concerning pains. As my outpatient GI's office is in the same wing of this hospital, I envisioned I'd be appearing at an OB clinic like Dr. Greenberg's. But, instead, this floor turned out to be the labor and delivery triage unit, which felt rather like an ER for pregnant women.

I began to feel scared, changing into a gown on a gurney in a small room with enough medical equipment to give me a sense of claustrophobia.

"Are you feeling the baby moving?" they'd asked me.

I placed my hand on my belly and focused.

"Not right now," I'd said.

"When was the last time you felt movement?"

Bipolar and Pregnant

I thought I'd cry. I couldn't remember. It's not something I was in the habit of paying attention to. Why were they asking this, when I came in for a problem with my digestive tract?

Before I finished tying the dumb strings at the top of the back of my gown, a nurse came in, asked me to lean back and relax, and placed two big round monitors on my belly—which was even more distended than usual.

"These monitor the baby's heartbeat and signs of contractions," she explained.

Seeing the baby's steady, quick and perfect little heartbeat helped me relax.

The nurse exited but shortly returned with two others. One of them explained they needed to do a pelvic exam, and I explained I have PTSD and always take a benzo before them.

Four days later, I was discharged from the hospital, having had either a partial small bowel obstruction, severe constipation, or, most likely, both.

Pretty much, what all happened in those four days were a blur. I remember two pelvic exams in the triage room, both of which made me sob and feel the exact same horror of violation I felt when I was raped. Even with a gentle healthcare professional barely touching me. Even with ten years passing between now and that ineffably shattering day.

I don't remember being moved upstairs to a regular room in the maternity wing. I remember a whole host of different doctors—a GI team, a maternal-fetal medicine team, a surgical team—coming in over those four days, and I remember crying often.

I can't rely on my memory, but I feel like I was asked countless times if I could feel the baby moving. Each time, I felt panicky. Could I feel her? When was the last time I felt her? Why did they keep asking me this?

I saw a psychiatrist in the hospital. I'm not sure why—maybe I'd had a panic attack, maybe they noticed the slew of psychiatric meds I was on—but someone asked me if I wanted a psychiatrist to see me.

"Yes," I said, gratefully.

Sometime later that day, Dr. Green, who had to have been younger than me, came in. With all my blurry thoughts—partly due to extreme stress, partly due to painkillers—I remembered what to be sure to tell him.

"I have bipolar disorder," I told the young man. "I've heard that steroids can trigger episodes."

I told Dr. Green how, twice in the past with IV steroids for acute Crohn's obstructions, I've had strong reactions of severe agitation and inexplicable crying—a reaction even common to patients without any mental health diagnoses. Already struggling with a depression episode and the anxiety that accompanies mine, I felt particularly vulnerable to a bad reaction to them.

There are many different medications that can instigate or exacerbate bipolar disorder episodes, not to mention the interactions that other drugs can have with bipolar medications. I think it's very important to both do your own research on potential side effects or interactions of new drugs—even ones used for a very short time—*and* obviously talk to your psychiatrist about them as soon as possible.

Bipolar and Pregnant

Dr. Green suggested what I'd also read can be helpful to counteract this response—an increase in benzos. He said he'd monitor me during my hospitalization, and I do remember him coming back to see me again.

Now, I had intense anxiety, painkillers, and benzos all messing with my mind and ability to feel like I was living in the present moment and make decisions or respond rationally. Eric's presence beside me helped a great deal, and I felt comforted knowing he was able to better keep track of how things were progressing during my hospitalization.

Glad as I was Eric was there, I was also annoyed, because he was supposed to be at his cousin's wedding, far out of town. I was upset that he was missing an event he had been looking forward to because of me, and I felt like a useless hindrance keeping him from it.

Finally, I made a turn for the better and was discharged home.

When I return in about twelve weeks to delivery the baby, will it feel like the same blurry bad dream?

Chapter 8. Weeks 29-32

At the beginning of Week 29, I saw Dr. Hillary Hanson again. Her office building is so much more unsettling than Dr. C's. Hers is a bona fide psychiatric clinic on one of the floors in one of the wings within a huge medical center, with "Psychiatry" in large letters in the hall by the entrance. To me, her office screams of mental *illness*, and this puts me on edge and sucks a bit of hope from my soul.

In stark contrast, Dr. C works out of a nice professional building, sharing a floor with small companies in finance and engineering and the like, where I'm always greeted by a pretty blonde receptionist with an Eastern European accent, high heels, and a short skirt.

"I will let him know you've arrived. Please, take a seat," she always offers, gracefully swooping her hand out toward some black leather armchairs before a table with a fresh copy of the *Robb Report*.

I approached the reception counter in Hanson's waiting room.

"I'm here to see Dr. Hanson," I said. "I have a 9:30 appointment."

"Name and photo ID," the woman grumbled, not looking up from her computer. She sighed as I produced my driver's license, glanced at it and then me, and handed it back. Apparently, there must be some fun-loving folks out there who go around stealing identities and impersonating others in their doctors' appointments.

"You can take a seat," she said. I turned around and quickly scanned for the vinyl-cushioned chair furthest away from anyone else in the large waiting room and sat down, wondering when the last time it was sprayed with effective disinfecting surfactants. I don't have OCD or anything, but one can't help but notice all the Xeroxed notices plastered on the walls saying, "Cover Your Cough" and "Cubra Su Tos", complete with stick-figure diagrams, for those illiterate in both languages I suppose. Or maybe too distracted by internal voices so as to need a visual representation of the advisement, this being the apt locale for visitors without the most streamlined thinking.

From my chair, I noticed two framed documents, again one in English and one in Spanish, on the wall opposite me. Having just gone over and signed the health care proxy with Eric that my OB's office gave me in case I become incapable of my own medical decisions in labor and delivery, I thought about these framed documents. "Patient Rights and Responsibilities," the header read.

I have been placed on involuntary psychiatric holds before—after my suicide attempts years ago. Incontestably deemed a danger to myself, I've been detained in a hospital under legal conditions designed to keep me safe while still affording me the most extensive personal liberties that didn't permit myself to harm myself.

As traumatizing as I felt being hospitalized was, I think that losing some of my personal freedoms there—like being able to wear a hoodie with a nice long drawstring (capable of self-strangulation?) or to use a shaving razor, like being able to shut myself in the bathroom or anywhere out of sight to sob privately for more than fifteen minutes before a staff member confirmed and documented my safe presence, like being able to—gosh—*leave* and go *home*—losing these were undoubtedly far less traumatizing than what I could have and likely would have done to myself if I hadn't been held.

Don't get me wrong—being contained behind locked doors isn't a cakewalk for the psyche, especially for someone like me and probably most of the others in the patient rooms down the hall from mine who had been victimized in physical or sexual abuse.

You don't have to have a history of trauma for involuntary containment to be scary. Do you know what is one of the most common reasons why the elderly consistently fall short of flu vaccination goals as a group, despite their manifold encounters with health care providers recommending it? Next to poor understanding of exactly what the vaccination is and does, this demographic, with all their uncontrollable problems and pains of aging within an increasingly confusing and impersonal healthcare system, say no to the flu shot simply because they can. They just want some control over themselves as patients.

I have never been forced to undergo any treatments for my mental health. Every pill I've swallowed has ultimately been a choice. Patients haven't always had this right.

While I've never refused to take medication inpatient, I did refuse repeated recommendations by Dr. Douglas to undergo electroconvulsive therapy (ECT) at Springview this past summer. I was grateful for this right.

What do you think of when you think of ECT? I can guess what a lot of you think, and I'll give you a hint: It won the 1976 Oscar for Best Picture (and Best Actor, Best Actress, Best Director, Best Adapted Screenplay…). *One Flew over the Cuckoo's Nest* was released at such a pivotal time in psychiatry, with the nation's heightened distrust of authority, and deinstitutionalization underway from Kennedy's "Community Mental Health Act", yet on the cusp of an unforeseen tsunami of psychiatric

Bipolar and Pregnant

problems in returning Vietnam vets, overwhelming the hospitals that remained, and eventually leaving so many homeless without asylum when the community centers meant to serve them were defunded. On the one hand, the movie resounded the cry for humanization of warehoused and maltreated patients, ensuring the patient rights on these framed documents I enjoy today. On the other hand, the award-winning film has proven to be a stalwart influence on public perception of psychiatry, with particularly extreme negative beliefs about ECT persisting.

You might not know that ECT is effective for both acute mania *and* acute depression. It's also safe in pregnancy. While many drugs can rapidly improve mania, depressions, unfortunately, tend to respond slowly to the medications used to treat them. Its safety, relatively quick effectiveness, and well-tolerated [for most, that is] side effect profile make it understandably a viable option to be considered in suicidal depression. Just like I had in D5.

But even then, wishing for death nearly every day there in Springview in D5, I persistently refused ECT and finally asked that it never be brought up again. Again, being the Not A Doctor that I am, I can only imagine the dilemma I put Dr. Douglas in. There I was, as painfully low as conceivable, desperate for relief, but yet refusing what might have been the safest and most efficient relief.

I wasn't afraid of the procedure, being a Jack Nicholas fan nonetheless. I fear the common side effect of retrograde amnesia. While I could make a joke here about how not being able to remember some time in severe depression could be beneficial, memory problems is no laughing matter to me. My pervading problems with memory and dissociation after my trauma were to me the most painful part of my Still Being Alive. I felt as though I were silenced underwater, my vision with an ever-decreasing aperture, the lens focusing sharply and rapidly on various somatic and mostly visceral memories of horror.

Maybe ECT would have helped me recover faster in D5. Maybe it would have prevented some or a lot of the pain I endured in choosing to wait for improvement. But I simply couldn't imagine the coexistence of a healthier mood with any memory problems similar to the disorientation and dissociation still worse, I thought, than that current severe D5 episode.

I was able to make a decision, though I don't know if I was able to communicate my reasoning to Dr. Douglas. I understand why he had been continuing to recommend it—clearly I was unwell, and compassionate persuasion is not the same as coercion. So when I, while not thinking at my clearest but having not lost touch with reality either, demanded it be removed as an option, that was the last I heard of it.

I had a rational reason for refusing ECT. But what if I didn't and what if I refused any and all medications too? Do you think there is an ethical dilemma in letting me languish on in suicidality?

Do you think there is an ethical dilemma in permitting bipolar patients to refuse treatment who experience psychosis in either their depression or manic episodes? When they are not acting in their best interests because of the illness itself, should others be able to become surrogates to hold their wellbeing for them until they are again able to?

Could mental health care providers work better with bipolar patients during times of wellness to set up an agreeable treatment plan in the case of mental incapacity, perhaps creatively using health care proxies or advance care directives? Would patients who are given the opportunity to explicitly direct psychiatrists on a legal document how they want to receive treatment when they are incapacitated and refusing it actually feel more in control of their illness?

The system isn't perfect for keeping people safe. Simply stated, with any patient freedoms, there are patient risks.

Remember my friend Daniel whose bipolar disorder was terminal? Daniel committed suicide while inpatient.

I've read that there is a heightened risk of suicide the days following inpatient discharge. I understand what this risk *feels* like because I remember waging war with the strong desire to end my life so many days in Springview in D5. I wanted them to unlock the back door, leading out to a grassy lawn, so that I could run down the wooded hillside, to where a passenger train would soon come, so I could step in front of it. But every one of those days, I effectually signed my name on a health care proxy, over to Dr. Douglas and his wonderful staff. When asked if I was having suicidal thoughts, I wrote my signature again and again, permitting them to keep that back door locked, keep checking on my safety all throughout the day and night, keep my medications safely stored away from my access, just by making the choice to say the truth: "yes".

Daniel became unable to write his name anymore.

Seeing those framed documents of patient rights on the wall, I was awash with gratefulness for those rights I get to enjoy today which were not always granted to patients just like me. I was thankful for the things in my life not controlled by me that have enabled me to live freely, out in the world, with my wonderful community. For Eric. For each of my family members; though we are broken apart, they each love me and would do anything to help me. For my financial resources, my education, my community of friends. All these gifts I have that I haven't earned in any way but have made the difference between me being the patient with bipolar disorder and PTSD living so richly and the homeless vagabond with bipolar disorder and PTSD under the bridge I drove on to get myself to this appointment that I was starting to complain about the moment I walked in the door.

Dr. Hanson appeared around the corner, and with mutual eye contact and soft smiles, I followed this expert with probably about the most excellent experience and education as I could find in the country to her office, where I discussed the very best evidence-based and personalized care with her.

Having had only just a few moments of quiet thankfulness in the waiting room, I was able to lay down some of my steely armor and recognize that not only an expert but a warm ally was sitting across from me. One who had the kind patience for me to find my words and who expressed understanding and acceptance in return. One who verbalized in no uncertain words that she cared about my problems and was concerned about helping me improve, whose body language probably was also communicating this all the while I set my default gaze to the floor to keep my tears held back. An ally I had become thankful for.

Eric is out of town for work for two weeks. Fortunately, he doesn't travel often for work—something I'll especially appreciate when I am alone caring for a baby.

This week, the vet called with good news: Lucky's surgery was a success. The tumor was excised, with clean margins, and the pathologist said it was not an aggressive growth. I was so relieved. I want to have many more years with Lucky. I don't know what I'd have done if the news came back bad, and I don't know how I'd have handled it alone at home, without Eric to lean on.

Bipolar and Pregnant

I saw Dr. Greenberg this week. The hospital set up the appointment last week when I was discharged.

Dr. Greenberg entered the room. She asked how I was doing since the hospital, and I told her that, other than awful diarrhea (sorry, Dear Diary), I felt fine.

Dr. Greenberg asked me to lie down so she could measure my belly. From the pubic bone to the top of the uterus, the measurement in centimeters should be within about two centimeters from the number of weeks pregnant you are. The baby is about the size of a butternut squash. Even at only 29 weeks, she would have a good chance of survival if born even this prematurely. I hope to keep growing her safe and strong, until it's just the right time for her to come out.

"You came to see me there, right? That stay was a blur. But you came by?"

Dr. Greenberg is always sunny and has a fabulous sense of humor. But her face turned serious. She nodded, slowly.

"You...were having a rough time." She stretched the tape over my ever-rising belly, which extends directly in front of me like an inflated basketball.

"What do you mean?" I said, confused. She told me I'd been crying.

I sat up, panic creeping in. I asked her if I'd seen her bedside, but she said she'd met me in the floor's family room.

I don't even remember anything at all about a family room — whether one existed or why in the world I'd have been in it.

"Well, you know, those couple of days were blurry because I was on pain medications," I said, more to myself than her, and changed the subject.

But after the appointment was over, I felt devastated. If memory problems only occurred with certain medications, I wouldn't be so bothered. But, looking over my past ten years of life, stress-induced dissociation causes a more profound problem with memory than anything. And to me this is very, very troubling.

If I can't keep track of what is going on around me, how am I supposed to take care of a baby?

Simply stated, I am unreliable.

Having come to terms with the fact that I had been suffering through my sixth depression, again with its unpredictable onslaught, I became more convinced that the best way for me to care for my baby is to ensure it will never need to be reliant upon me. I need the assurance that, if I become incapable of keeping up with life—first the accessories of hobbies and social entertainments; next the expectations of work and of household manager; then the basics of daily self-care; and finally, the ability to simply allow for life to be sustained without giving in to the desire to end it—if these disappear then I have to hold the security that I've done my best to protect my baby from the harms I'd be inflicting on Eric in my progressive desertion.

I came to realize that I should not breastfeed. Breastfeeding our baby is something only I can do, and I don't want to start her out with something I might not be able to continue. My friend at church had to spend a day at the hospital getting a kidney stone removed, and her infant refused a bottle. Because I'm simply not going to be able to breastfeed every other hour, all through the night too, I already intended and discussed with Eric introducing the bottle right away for some of her feeds. What if she dislikes going back and forth between breast and bottle and this adds stress to Eric, trying to feed her with it? What if I can't keep up with demands through pumping? What if it turns out I have to rely on a bottle and formula more than expected, and I feel even worse about this? Wouldn't it be easier if I drop any expectations that I can breastfeed?

At least with formula in a bottle, the unsettling unknowns are removed, and I have assurance of a plan.

Maybe my mental health will be okay after the baby arrives. But, maybe being the best mother I can be means working off of not what I hope to be able to do but what I'm assured I'll be able to do.

But I have no assurance I'll be able to do *anything* right for this baby. I might be utterly useless. Or worse: a burden.

I told Holly the next week at our appointment about how upset I was over not being able to remember my recent hospital stay — conversing with Dr. Greenberg there or the progression of events from admission to discharge.

Dissociation — drug-related or not — terrifies me. The awareness of its recent presence is enveloped in the same sense of powerlessness and aloneness that constitute the core ingredients of trauma. And this makes me feel utterly unfit to be a mother.

I also told Holly that I was really upset at Eric for staying home from his cousin's wedding to be with me in the hospital. He missed his mom's birthday to stay near me during D5, and we also had to cancel our plans to have my mom and her husband out to visit for July 4th during D5. I kept wrecking all of our plans.

I told Holly how I'd noticed I was a little angry (yay for New Year's resolutions) but that that didn't persuade Eric to fly off to the wedding.

"That is great of Eric!" Holly responded. Holly, my unconditionally warm, non-judgmental therapist, rarely makes judgment statements and advice like this, so I listened up.

"Do you see how he was taking care of you?" she asked. "He recognized what you needed, even when you didn't see it. Even if it meant you were going to be upset with him, he cared more right then about taking the best care of you."

"Yeah..." I admitted, reluctantly. I can be stubborn, but Holly did have a good point. It still didn't sit well, but I took a moment and thoughtfully had to agree with her. "I was pretty disoriented. I guess I would have felt really lost without him there at the hospital with me."

That must have been really difficult for Eric. Being the people-pleaser that I can be, I don't know if I could have held strong in the moment, if I were in his shoes. But this example of his dependability gave me encouragement. It gave me hope, for being there for Baby, even when times come where I can't.

That week, in Week 30, with Eric still away, I was in a car wreck. Returning home from the grocery store on the freeway, the cars in front of me braked quickly. I had been focused on the road—it was raining—and was able to brake in time to avoid the sedan in front of me. But in my rearview mirror, I saw the unavoidable.

An SUV skidded and smashed right into the back of my car. The sound of metal-on-metal was so loud that I expected to turn around and find my entire trunk accordioned into the back seat.

Bipolar and Pregnant

My hands were shaking, and I hit my hazard lights. The car behind me remained still, and from my mirror I could see a woman holding out her cell phone and then putting it to her ear.

I found my phone and dialed Eric, who responded right away.

"Eric," I began, coaching myself to relax, "I've just been in an accident. I was rear-ended." I kept him on the phone as I calmly told him I was scanning my whole body. I was okay. I didn't hit anything. It all happened so quickly, but I don't think my stomach hit the wheel.

I hung up with Eric. I didn't need to jump right to taking photos and exchanging information and calling the police department. I just took some slow, gentle breaths, my hands shaking, then still, placed in front of me on the wheel.

The woman behind me was uninjured as well, though her car also had damage albeit not nearly as bad as mine. But a car is trivial. I was okay. This kind, apologetic woman was okay. And, as far as I could guess, the baby was okay.

When I had made it the short distance home, I called the OB office. Since it was a Saturday, the on-call OB returned her page and asked me to come to the medical center for a check-up. She wanted me to arrive at the same location I had arrived at only two weeks ago, with my GI pain.

This time, I remained calm upon arrival. I had been purposefully paying attention to the baby's movements and was able to tell them that they seemed normal. After a brief rest on a gurney with those same two fetal heartbeat and maternal contraction monitors, they sent me home.

At home, after a soothing shower, snuggled on the sofa in cozy clothes with cancer-free Lucky sleeping by my side, I was distracted from the book I was reading. Remember that week of mayhem with those three events when I was 22? The hospitalization (like I've just had), the car wreck (today), and the roommate's crazy ex-boyfriend? Well, I'm pretty sure Eric isn't going to go attacking any of his exes, but I was reminded afresh of how I felt during those three events over ten years ago.

It got me thinking about resiliency. Something both Holly and my old therapist Lindsay have said to me is that I have tremendous resilience. Both times, I had to laugh. Were they not listening to me all this time where I've talked about myself? How I crack apart, how the gentlest of winds knock me over?

Maybe this is what prompted Lindsay to assign Judith Herman's *Trauma* book to me to read. Reading this book, and discussing it with Lindsay each week as I read it, felt like being *known* by the author. I had never understood how very well others understand the problems I had after being raped. To learn that my problems were not personal failings but common effects I'd bravely been battling without much help gave me a modicum of acknowledgement that, yes, I might actually have some resiliency in me.

It's easy for me to forget this. To focus on the ways I can't keep up, the ways I can't adjust and regroup and *relax*.

I remember the first time Holly called me resilient, and my little laugh was followed by my emphatic disagreement. At the time of that session with her, I'd been especially struggling; durable was the opposite of how I felt.

"But you *are* very strong, and you have tremendous resources. They're just not all accessible right now," she said. Then Holly, using an analogy of an army of soldiers to fight a war, explained something that made me think of the "complex" PTSD that Herman had written about. I have an abundance of soldiers,

Bipolar and Pregnant

Holly reiterated, but nearly all of them are constantly fighting, and some of the battles have been going on for a very long time.

Maybe she was talking about the chronic physical abuse as a child; I still am and probably always will be guarded. Maybe soldiers are perpetually making peace treaties and making sure everyone keeps their pins in their grenades; I still tend to be a peace-seeking buffer. Soldiers might be fighting the disbelief I had of my parents' divorce and the unspeakable circumstances that led to it.

I'll never know, but maybe if I'd had more soldiers available, I'd have been able to seek help after being raped.

Maybe I've gotten through some difficult battles. But I don't feel resilient.

Eric, on the other hand, seems extremely resilient to me. On the sofa with my sleeping Lucky, the slow rise and fall of her chest as she breathes making my heart melt into the sweetest love for this little animal, I thought about how I've been able to garner strength from Eric. It was Eric who helped keep me afloat in that completely hazy hospital stay. It was Eric who I could dial to be there on the line as a safety net for me if I started to fall apart.

With Eric, I'm able to process things so much better than before, when I was a single woman. I have Eric to talk to and express my emotions to and feel supported by. He's my safe person.

I want to be this safe person for our daughter. I want her to feel like her tall mom's feet are planted on the bottom of the pool, so she's safe to swim without fear. That I'm able to see her, that I'm able to reach her, and that I'm able to swim after her if she's gone to waters she's not ready for yet.

I want to be an anchor and a haven. I want to be her Mom, who is always there for her and loves her unconditionally.

But I'm so afraid I can't be this.

I'm afraid I'll be something my daughter has to overcome. I'm afraid I'll be holding her back—that I'll be the one floundering in the pool—me, the mom with mental illness, who might scare her and worry her and upset her.

What if I'm the mom who just isn't there for her?

My insecurities only grew that weekend, in Week 31. Eric had finished his out-of-state work assignment, and I flew there to meet him. The trip was meant to be our "babymoon"—our last little romantic getaway before having the baby.

However, most of the trip was spoiled. Eric met me at the airport, and we went straight to dinner.

The office there had offered him a job. He had been weighing out a couple different options before the trip, each of which I was trying to wrap my head around as my future home, but this city hadn't really been on our radar. Moreover, the other options would be for a move a few months after the baby is born, but this move would likely be much sooner. He was very excited about the promotion offer. He'd even booked a showing of a house for us to see.

Eric makes decisions quickly. I tend to take my time, needing to give things a good chew. I can't even describe how I make decisions because there is so much abstract processing involved, in which intuition and emotions play a role. Eric's processes, on the other hand, are linear and systematic. He could probably lay forth his processes in a beautiful flow chart; in fact, he may have

Bipolar and Pregnant

already done this at some point in his spare time, this being exactly the type of project he'd find pleasure in.

Suitcase at my side—we hadn't even left the airport yet, this was all too fast for me.

We—though this was beginning to feel more like *I*—still had ten more weeks of pregnancy. Plus several more weeks postpartum to get used to taking care of her and adjust to a drastic change in my daily life and sleep schedule. The sleep schedule that Holly and Eric and I had been so careful to plan ahead for. The adequate sleep that was my best defense at staving off the high risk I'd be in for having a postpartum bipolar episode.

Planning to get adequate sleep in the postpartum has required thoughtful exercise for me and Eric, with Holly helping too. The massive sleep disturbances combined with the dramatic hormonal changes after giving birth and caring for a newborn are the main two ingredients for the recipe for postpartum depression. The hormones I can't control, but the sleep is somewhat in my jurisdiction.

Setting up a personal system to ensure adequate sleep is one thing, but figuring out how to protect sleep while also taking care of the round-the-clock needs of a newborn is another thing altogether. Eric decided to take four weeks off from work after the baby arrives, and we decided not to have any guests—however helpful they might want to be—until after this time, to help ease us into a schedule that works for us.

This is likely going to be a trial-and-error process, and, being the person who craves predictability, it's a little stressful to contemplate the unknowns of the feasibility of our plan. But our blueprint looks pretty good. We decided to break the night into shifts. Eric will take the first feeds, and then I'll cover the ones the rest of the night. Or vice versa. We are keeping a bed in the nursery, for each of us to sleep in until we tag-team. Eric picked out a baby monitor where alerts are only sent if the baby's noise reaches a certain decibel, so that every little coo doesn't startle me awake and jolt me upright.

I'll also try to nap when the baby sleeps in the day. Unlike Eric, who can fall asleep at will, any time and any place, in under five minutes, I have difficulty taking naps. However, I have been trying to take some naps in pregnancy and usually manage one or two a week, for about an hour. It's a luxury of not being employed.

How do bipolar working moms get enough sleep? How do bipolar working *single* moms?

Beyond all the challenges of being bipolar and pregnant, the "fourth trimester" after pregnancy is the most demanding of physical, psychological, and emotional resources; the postpartum period is when I'll be most vulnerable.

So when Eric began talking about moving in this critical period of time, I got scared. I rely on him to be the rock. The steady one. The one that talks sense into me when I don't take my health needs seriously.

I drew inward. The unknowns of the near future left me feeling very insecure. The unsettledness of things around me made me panic, already having so much instability within me.

My self-confidence fell significantly. I began assuming I'd be absolutely useless in caring for a newborn. I counted all of my vulnerabilities and special needs—like needing help with overnight feeds—as evidence that I was going to be—actually that I already *was*—a failure of a mother.

That I was worthless.

Bipolar and Pregnant

The same week, Week 31, after we returned home, I saw Dr. Greenberg—but first, nurse Greta. She asked me if I had signed up for the birthing class at my hospital.

"No," I told her. "But I read about the basics of labor and delivery." She nodded her approval.

I had asked some of my mom friends about their experiences with birth classes, and I mostly got negative reviews. Everything they wanted to know turned out to simply be online, and skipping the birth class would allow you to skip listening to everyone's horror-inducing questions about worst-case hypotheticals. Not for me.

"What about the breastfeeding class?" she asked, typing away at her computer.

"No, I'm going to formula feed."

Silence from the keyboard. Greta looked to me as though I'd just told her I was planning to rob the bank on my lunch break. Maybe rob it naked.

I tried to explain to her that I wanted the baby to have consistency, that I wouldn't be able to exclusively breastfeed, and that Eric would need to help out with overnight feedings.

"The hospital won't have bottles or formula for the baby," she said. "They'll want you to be breastfeeding, and they don't even have them there."

"That seems ridiculous," I said. "What about all the women who *can't* breastfeed?"

Like bipolar women taking lithium, for one.

"Only one in one thousand women can't breastfeed," she said, with an insistent little huff.

"You gave me a folder at a previous appointment on all the labor and delivery information from the hospital. It specifically said that those who choose to formula feed would be given support," I said. Not only had I read that, I had specifically shown that line in the patient folder to Eric, when we were discussing formula feeding.

"I don't think so," Greta said, incredulously. "It's part of being a baby-friendly hospital," she said. "And the baby will be with you the whole time; the hospital has a rooming-in policy because it's a baby-friendly hospital."

Holly had told me about this rooming-in policy, and this was also mentioned in the folder Greta had given me and was on the hospital's website, nicely tucked under the patient resources section, which of course I read. Holly had explained that rooming-in might be the default for the hospital's maternity floor but that I'd be able to use the nursery because I have a medical need for it. I was planning to ask Dr. Hanson, next time I see her, about how to be sure my baby can sleep at the nursery when I sleep.

"Yes," I answered Greta. "I know about rooming-in and know that I'll need to use the nursery. I am planning to ask my psychiatrist to put in a doctor's order to be able to use it. Because with bipolar disorder I can't go a night without sleep."

"Well, you don't need a doctor's order…You can just request it. But they want you to keep the baby with you, and they'll want you to breastfeed."

"So if they don't have bottles or formula in the hospital, I'll need to bring my own?" I asked.

"Yes," she said. "You'll need to bring your own."

I didn't say anything, but I inwardly rolled my eyes at this nurse who had just lost pretty much all credibility with me.

When Greta left the room, as I waited for Dr. Greenberg, a quick search on my phone for what a "baby-friendly hospital" is led me to several articles, one being from my city's major newspaper, that talked about the abounding complaints new mothers had about rooming-in policies and other components of the Baby-Friendly Hospital Initiative. The articles told of women—women who had given birth at my same hospital—who felt shamed by staff and were denied access to the nursery even when they clearly needed some help after exhausting labors.

My heart sank.

The initiative was created by the World Health Organization and UNICEF in the early 90's to increase the success rate of breastfeeding, and it has been picking up a lot of traction in the U.S.—and recently, the city I live in. Immediate skin-to-skin contact in the hospital with the baby after delivery, as well as demand feeding, where mothers are near and well attuned to early hunger cues, improve the opportunity for breastfeeding to get off to a successful start. And a successful start helps ensure that women will continue breastfeeding when they go home.

I understand the correlation between rooming-in and higher rates of breastfeeding after hospital discharge. But where are the stats on rooming-in with postpartum depression, especially for those patients with risk factors for postpartum depression? As I've said over and over, the strongest trigger for an acute bipolar episode is sleep deprivation. And, P.S., depression, anxiety disorders, and PTSD can all likewise be triggered and exacerbated by inadequate sleep. Do you see how rooming-in sets many women off on a dangerous start?

Many women with mental health disorders sacrifice their own health, and in turn the health of their baby, out of undue fear and shame from [well-meaning] pushy nurses and lactation consultants and from public attitudes in order to breastfeed. It's great when initiatives "make the healthy choice the easy choice", but when the physical demands of breastfeeding and patient beliefs about a need for medication cessation for breastfeeding can severely exacerbate mental health disorders, there should be better patient-centered care to ensure that the healthiest choice isn't the most cumbersome, right?

I know the benefits of breastfeeding. I also know how very demanding it can be, and, as I've said, I'm afraid I won't be able to be reliable to keep up and that the baby needs other caregivers like Eric to be counted on for feeding. With my increased susceptibility to postpartum depression, I fear these demands would affect my ability to care for my baby.

For Baby and me, maybe breast is not best?

Greta returned to the room and retracted what she'd said about the unit not providing formula and bottles, but she did say that the hospital team would also talk with me about breastfeeding and strongly promote it, as well as rooming-in.

I wished I had known my hospital was a baby-friendly one, because I probably would have chosen a different one if I'd known about these policies. With sleep imperative to my mental health, will my medical needs—and in turn, my baby's—be in jeopardy when I deliver?

Bipolar and Pregnant

I'm already so insecure about motherhood. Will my medical providers on my baby's birth day give me support, or shame? Will I start out motherhood even more heavily burdened by my bipolar disorder?

In Week 32, Eric and I had a family meeting with Holly. We discussed sleep strategies and postpartum care—how to get support when needed, as well as the warning signs and symptoms of postpartum depression. We also discussed Eric's job decision, with Holly using most of our time to help us come up with strategies to make a move easier—especially if it comes soon after Baby.

All these plans we're setting in place should make me feel reassured. But instead, they just make me feel like our baby will have to overcome *me*.

Eric probed me about my low confidence a few nights later.

"I don't understand why you feel like you don't measure up," he said. "Please be honest with me here: Do you feel like I give you enough validation?"

"Yes, you do," I replied, without hesitation, and I meant it.

He looked puzzled. And I felt puzzled too.

"I don't know why I feel so inadequate for motherhood, besides my fears with bipolar disorder," I admitted. "But it isn't related to lack of support from you."

"Are you sure?"

I hated that he felt to blame for the low self-esteem I was carrying around.

I told him how I'd studied anorexia nervosa in my dietitian training and how these patients had a pervasive intractable belief that they were too fat. I explained that, no matter how many times others had told them before their weight loss that they were beautiful as they were, and no matter how low the number on the scale got, they believed everyone was wrong and that they needed to lose more weight.

A delusional perception driving a never-ending losing effort for the unattainable. And one that came from within.

After church on Sunday, Eric told me he'd reflected on my insecurity, and we had a great spiritual talk. One of the best things about marriage is that the intimacy gives your spouse the ability to see things you can't. Our marriage gives Eric and me the opportunity to show each other ways we can apply spiritual truths from the Bible to our lives, right in the context of our particular circumstances.

We talked about my identity and how it affects my behaviors. How do I see myself? Eric and I both know the answer to this, and since you've been reading my otherwise private thoughts, you know a lot about how I see myself too.

There are two critical concepts in Christianity that I sometimes fail to distinguish in my mind, which greatly hinders my spiritual life with God.

In one concept, there is a union I have with Jesus Christ that is permanent. Because of my faith in Jesus who paid my punishment, I believe God sees me with the approval of the perfect life Jesus earned for me. This is based on one of my favorite verses in the Bible—Romans 3:23-24, which says, "for all have sinned and fall short of the glory of God, being *justified* as a gift by his grace through the redemption which is in Jesus Christ." This happened when I put my faith in the gospel—

Christian salvation. It can't be lost by anything bad I do, and it can't be improved upon by anything good I do; God promises to continually forgive and love me and consider me his own. This is the freedom God wants me to live life in.

The other concept is a process, not a one-time change. It is the gradual changes I make in my life to follow the Bible, to become more like the person Jesus was. Because God's love for me is based on my unity with Christ, I should continually strive to be like Christ in our unity. It isn't a requirement for God's forgiveness but an *effect* of it. It's a transformation, sometimes slow, sometimes fast. It is how faith grows.

Eric showed me how my Christian growth was being impeded by my feelings of worthlessness. If I really believed I was the person God saw me as—a justified and loved child with a life worth living, my defeated spirit would be changed. I'd have more hope about the future and more confidence as someone who didn't have to live up to whatever unattainable ideals I'd formed for myself as a mother with bipolar disorder.

What Eric showed me was deeply moving. I regularly read my Bible, and Eric and I are active members of our church. I practice spiritual disciplines to help grow my faith, and I can see ways I've changed a whole lot over the past years. But what Eric was showing me was a spiritual problem that I'd failed to see as clearly as he was showing me.

This is the very best part about marriage.

It's imperative that Christians like me understand that these concepts of change are distinct. It's how I can tell you that I'm a Christian and loved by God, but that I still struggle with all the human battles an imperfect and stubbornly pessimistic person fights and often loses.

It's why I still struggle with worries and fears. It's why I still find reasons to believe I'm not up for the job of being a mom. It's why I still peer down the corridors of time and see the heartaches of mental illness awaiting me and how this causes me to balk and assume the worst.

On the last day of Week 32, my church threw me a big baby shower. The two ladies I meet with weekly—Rita and Lily—helped coordinate it. Even being on a weekday night, well over half of all the women in our church came. My nursery room décor has clouds with colorful raindrops, so they had decorated the otherwise blank and totally white reception hall with big white tissue paper clouds and about a million colorful raindrops on the walls, complete with artistically placed umbrellas and a beautiful display of refreshments. It was all a bit enchanting.

I opened gift after gift after gift. My little sister Aubrey with her toddler and baby twins helped me create a gift registry and was invaluable in helping me focus on things that were essential and efficient. If anyone would know about practicality in baby products, it's her.

The mountain of baby gifts was overwhelming. But even more so, looking out at the dozens of women there, enjoying the shower, doting on me, and celebrating the upcoming arrival of my baby, was humbling. Four women made quilts for the baby—quilts that looked like a lot of time and love had been stitched into them. And three of these four women I hardly knew at all. They say it takes a village to raise a child. I was awash with emotion for the love and support Eric and I have as we enter parenthood.

Bipolar and Pregnant

We are likely moving out of state in a few months, with whichever position Eric decides to pursue. I will miss all these women at church and their families. I'll miss my neighbors, and all my other friends like Cat and my run club.

I found out I was pregnant right after I found out I had bipolar disorder. As I told you, Eric and I used contraception again right after Dr. C told me I was hypomanic and needed to start taking lithium. If those two lines hadn't appeared on my pregnancy test a few days after I was discharged from Springview, I probably wouldn't be pregnant today. I'd have wanted to hold off on having a baby, maybe until I'd had a long period of stability, or maybe I'd always feel unprepared and the desire for children would slip away.

But maybe the timing was actually perfect. What had seemed like an impossible challenge has caused me to rely on others more—others like all the wonderful families at my baby shower, others like Holly and Dr. C, like Eric for sure, and like God. Maybe recognizing that I need and will need help as a woman living with bipolar disorder has allowed me to recognize the help I'll need from our community and family as Eric and I raise our baby.

Eric helped me bring all the gifts that filled the back of our SUV into our home. Scattered around the baby's room were clothing and burp cloths and books and toys, teething rings and onesies and booties and blankets. I leaned back in the rocking recliner and took it all in.

This is all real.

And she'll be here real soon.

Katie McDowell

Chapter 9. Weeks 33-36

I swam this week, in Week 33, at a nice indoor 50 meter pool I have membership access to through Eric's work. With my growing belly, I want to reduce my weight-bearing activity to ensure my back doesn't get too achy. I'm still able to run, with a maternity support belt helping to keep it comfortable, but, for now, running doesn't give me the expansive mindset and satisfaction from movement that it usually does. So I decided to take myself to the pool.

Wearing a two-piece workout suit beneath my clothes, I grabbed my gym bag and a special kickboard that Emma had gifted to me for a recent birthday, nearly identical to the one I had and loved when we were kids together. Kicking side-by-side in practice, we as little nine-year-olds grew our friendship that has withstood time and distance while holding kickboards just like the one in my hand, now a mature thirty-three-year-old with a little girl inside of me.

I opened the door to the natatorium, slightly warmer inside than outside on that crisp spring day, and an intense wave of emotion came over me. The smell of chlorine, the feel of humidity in the air, and the rhythmic sounds of swimmers moving their way through the water—I closed my eyes for a second to take it in.

Home.

Swimming was where I learned how to live life, and returning to the pool reminded me of the person I both once was and yet also somehow still am.

When I was a swimmer, I was fiercely tenacious. I never gave up, and I believed with all of my heart that I could achieve any goal I made if I worked hard enough. There were no limitations, and with these beliefs, I had no trepidation—only determination.

Was I naïve? Couldn't I see all the uncontrollable factors that would necessarily limit me? Why did I regard myself invincible?

In college swimming, I was awarded the Most Spirited award 2 years in a row. I cheered, I affirmed, and I found just the right words to uplift the downtrodden. I had a contagious enthusiasm that pulsated across the team and could turn any negative into a positive motivational force.

Why was I persistently optimistic? Was I blind to reality, or was my outward buoyancy concealing something inside?

Also in college, my teammates elected me to be their Team Captain. On a team with some of the fastest girls in the world, I was eons away from being their MVP. But my example of disciplined devotion, my steadiness in all seasons, and my careful attention to build up my teammates exemplified leadership qualities I wasn't even aware I possessed.

Where did this fortitude come from, and why did I ever believe I could actually be counted on for encouragement and motivation?

I have countless memories of swimming. When I met with Lindsay in grad school, I shared many of my favorites of them with her, doing my best to explain the sport as I went along.

One day, as we sat down to begin our time together, she asked me, "How was your weekend?"

"Great!" I replied. Then, reflexively, "Yours?"

"Good too." Then she paused, and with a twinkle in her eye, she grinned and shared a secret she'd been keeping as a part of the whole maintenance of professional boundaries that made our time together safe and secure.

"I was at swim meets all weekend," she said. "My kids are swimmers too."

I knew very little else about The Life of Lindsay, just as I only know a couple facts about Holly. But Lindsay's little disclosure that day helped us to draw upon the bottomless well of experiences and analogies I have from swimming, and I loved this.

It has been a dozen years since I competed, and I hardly ever go to the pool, so I don't often think of swimming anymore. But, as any trauma survivor knows, sensory reminders, like I experienced that day entering the pool in Week 33, are very powerful transports.

I put my bag on a bench, took my clothes and shoes off, and walked over to the starting end of the pool. I dipped a foot in, careful to maintain my balance with my pregnant body. Perfect temperature. I placed my silicon cap to my forehead and pulled it over my head, twirling up my ponytail and tucking it inside, like I've done literally thousands of times. Putting on my goggles, I slowly dipped myself into the pool. When I was ready, I positioned my feet on the wall underwater, dropped my body beneath the surface too, streamlined my arms, and pushed off, all with perfect muscle memory.

I absolutely loved swimming.

My college coach was not a jovial man. Frankly, he was usually quite a grump. But, having probably coached more women to

Bipolar and Pregnant

the Olympics than any other person in history, he knew the sport. I didn't need to be coached by a ray of sunshine. I needed someone who took swimming seriously; we were an excellent pair.

At the beginning of every season, Coach had long meetings with each of us on the team individually to discuss our goals. He expected us to write out the times we wanted to go and what we thought we needed to do in training to achieve them.

I remember one meeting when Coach rejected one of my goals and how it surprised me. I set lofty goals for myself. I wanted to make the Olympics, so I consistently aimed high. But I believed I never aimed *too* high; all the goals I wrote down to show Coach I fully believed I could achieve.

Coach and I were making our way down the list of events I swam and the goal times I'd made for them, but he stopped at the 200 freestyle. As I recall, I set my goal time two seconds faster than my best time, which, for a 200 when you're at an elite level, is a significant time drop.

"I don't think you can do this," he said.

But before I had time to even consider getting flustered with him and telling him why I thought I could, or maybe getting flustered with myself and feeling like I'd set delusional expectations for myself, Coach scrawled a line through my time on the paper and wrote a new time next to it, followed by a question mark. He handed the paper back to me.

His time was a full second faster than the one I'd written.

The time he wrote was achievable. That's what I came to believe. I brought him a revised goal sheet the next day, with the very fast time on it, with bullet points of what I'd need to change to earn it.

We went to work. I had a target, and I had a plan.

I went a personal best time that season, but I did not drop three, or even two, seconds in my 200 freestyle. But I remember it didn't matter that I didn't even get the goal I'd set—I was very proud of my hard work that season, and the following season Coach and I again wiped the goal sheet clean and started afresh with new exciting plans.

Swimming laps in Week 33, carrying a growing baby in my womb, I remembered the Katie I was as a swimmer. The fierce competitor, the spirited teammate, and the motivational leader. The young woman who didn't get discouraged easily, who simply felt gladness and pride from doing her best.

And I wanted to be like her again.

Things were changing. With less than two months until Due Date, motherhood was becoming more imminent, and I couldn't avoid my fears any longer. With my recent discussion with Eric on how my spiritual life was affecting my behaviors, I was freshly equipped with hope and spiritual strength. And my depression, I felt, had fully lifted by now; I felt like my Usual Self again and had the capacity to think and plan…and act.

What would the old Katie do?

I have a grave incurable illness. One that limits me. But bipolar disorder doesn't need to paralyze me. Focusing on all the uncontrollable problems that *could* occur postpartum wasn't helping me move forward like the old Katie would.

Bipolar and Pregnant

I needed goals, and I needed a plan. The overarching aim of being a good mother isn't as clear-cut as a swim time goal, but there were still things around me and within me that I wanted to improve, as a mother-to-be.

I thought about how I'd given up on the idea of breastfeeding out of pessimism. Breastfeeding—even if only temporarily after my baby was born—is something I've always wanted to do. The old Katie would give it a try. She'd arm herself with knowledge and a plan, and her self-esteem would remain intact just fine if it didn't work out, because she'd have done her best.

Could I try? Could I attempt breastfeeding right after delivery and give her the rich colostrum my body would make for her? Would it be possible to interchange breast and bottle, so that Eric could help with feeds, without going dry or without the baby refusing one or the other? Could I use some formula and some breast milk if I couldn't meet her demands or if pumping became too much of a burden for her mom's wellbeing?

I had learned about breastfeeding, but I decided to sign Eric and me up for my hospital's breastfeeding class as an interactive refresher, to boost my confidence, scheduled in Week 35. But then I considered my situation and how I'd have so many questions specific to it that probably wouldn't be answered in the class. I needed to talk to someone who could work with me like Coach and help me devise an individualized plan.

I emailed Dr. Marino's nurse and asked if the clinic had a lactation consultant I could make an appointment with. They didn't, so I called the OB office. I spoke with a nurse, and she scheduled an appointment in a couple weeks with a lactation consultant named Dr. Jessica Hartley.

I was on a proactive streak, and it felt good.

Of course I'm still afraid—of myself, of the future. Facing reality—fully accepting that I'm bipolar and pregnant—is scary. But I can start to feel prepared for motherhood by owning it now. The life inside me is my baby, and I am her mother.

I saw Dr. Greenberg this week. The last time I saw her, freshly disheartened by all the disorientation and panic I had in the hospital after barely being touched, I asked her if mental health problems were acceptable reasons to have an elective c-section.

I'm afraid that I'll be a dissociative freak show all throughout labor and delivery and that I won't be able to function when she arrives. I'm afraid I'll look back on her birth day as a reliving of a nightmare.

Dr. Greenberg and I talked more about the option. I'd assumed she'd be very biased against c-sections. I've read that in obstetrics there has been more of a push for labor (ha) instead of elective c-sections. This comes with good cause. The surgery typically has a much longer and more painful recovery than a vaginal delivery, and risk for infection of the uterus and at the incision are not unsubstantial factors.

We were also concerned about scar tissue and the formation of adhesions and whether that would affect my Crohn's disease. But I talked with my GI, and the location (ileal, not colonic) and nature (stricturing, not fistulizing) of my disease don't really predispose me to greater complications post-op than other women.

I wasn't too worried about the maternal complications of a c-section. Besides, I was even more focused on how the list of risks to my baby decreases with a c-section compared to a vaginal delivery. Maybe the argument could me made that natural would be safer for me, but I liked that c-section seems very safe for Baby.

Bipolar and Pregnant

Mostly, though, I love the idea of a set plan, where I have a much more measurable idea of the possible outcomes, unlike labor and delivery, where it seems like anything could happen, and where ultimately a c-section could end up being necessary. I'm no masochist (I plan to definitely have an epidural if I go through labor), but I'm not really afraid of the pain of having Baby the natural way. It's more of fear of the unknowns and the countless stressors I could face, in addition to the horrible triggers of being exposed and touched that I *would* face with labor. I'm afraid of whether I'd mentally be able to handle this.

Dr. Greenberg and I decided to go ahead and put my name on the surgical schedule. Dr. Greenberg will be out of town at that time, but that's okay—my major urban medical center I'm sure has excellent surgeons covering for her.

I marked the date and time in my calendar, scheduled for the first day of Week 40: Baby's Delivery.

A colossal weight lifted off my shoulders.

It's not to say I was doubt-free about the tentative plan. I met with Holly in Week 33, and we talked about it.

"I'm just not positive it's the right decision for me. I'm afraid I'd be making a decision based on fear, and fear-motivated decisions aren't always the best ones," I explained.

Holly understood, but she also commended me for being in tune with my own needs. I thought more about it, and I also just let it sit for a while.

Was I making a knee-jerk reaction to all the uncertainties around me? Could I mentally handle labor and delivery, and would I regret not trying?

Eric and I went to Baby's last ultrasound together at the end of Week 34. This late ultrasound was scheduled because that high-risk OB I saw months ago Dr. Rebekah Stein had recommended it since IBD is associated with impaired growth. However, my baby is growing great, weighing in at the 60th percentile, according to the ultrasound technician. She is so big now, weighing about 5 pounds 14 ounces.

Eric has pointed out more than once that I keep referring to our baby, which he calls by her [secret] name, as "it". "*She*," he corrects me. I did it again this week, and I felt bad. I've known for many weeks she's a girl now.

Have I subconsciously been avoiding her name because I'm afraid of her reality? Or is it because for so many weeks, before Emma's gender reveal party, I didn't know if she was a girl or boy and "it" just kind of stuck?

I started making an effort to consciously call her by her name at home, and to think of her as my baby girl, who will come out and have a mama soon. Now, I use her name so much that I'm afraid I'll slip the secret with my friends or family!

In actuality, I've been taking very good care of my daughter. I've been keeping all her appointments and doctors' advice, I've been following great nutrition, and I've adjusted my exercise habits to make sure her mom stays comfortable and injury-free. I've been reading about her development, different options to birth her, and how to best take care of her when she arrives.

In addition to using her name, instead of worrying I won't feel attached to her if I fall into a depression, I'm working on other ways to feel attached to her now already. I made something special with her name on it for her room. I also hand-stitched a

Bipolar and Pregnant

baby mobile for her crib—something that took a lot of time to do, my only artistic talent being poetry and not crafts like this.

Why does nesting feel so good? What's going on in my body that makes me feel so serene, as I rock in her room with one of her blankets, simply looking to her white crib, with her mobile of clouds hanging above it? Do these feelings just happen because of hormones, or can I cultivate them to last when my body changes and they go away?

I feel my baby moving in me all the time, but I don't usually imagine what she looks like inside—a baby—*my* baby moving. I've started to imagine what she'll look like when she arrives. Eric has enjoyed our musings together on this. We look very different from each other, and I've begun wondering which features of mine she'll inherit and which of Eric's. In contrast to my blonde hair and blue eyes, Eric has dark hair and dark eyes, and I've read that his are dominant traits. Maybe she'll have black hair, like my dad's; this thought makes me smile. She's a part of not solely Eric and me, but also the people we love.

First when I was alone, but now just as often with Eric, I talk to her when I feel her moving. I tell her I love her. I tell her I'll do my best for her.

In Week 35, Eric and I went to an infant care class at the medical center. We learned the basics of what to expect when Baby arrives and comes home with us, and we got to practice some basic care techniques like cleaning, dressing, diapering, burping, swaddling, and simply holding a baby. Because I've been volunteering in my churches' nurseries on a monthly rotation for a few years now—in grad school, in my clinical internship year, and now here in this city with Eric, I've had a lot of experience taking care of babies. But Eric doesn't really have any experience, so I signed us up for the class mostly for him.

Katie McDowell

What I found most helpful about the class were the guidelines of when to contact Baby's pediatrician. I suspect I'm going to worry about every little cough and low-grade fever and won't know whether I'm being an alarmist or am appropriately contacting Dr. Marino.

Will I be overly protective of our baby?

I think I worry my baby is especially vulnerable because she's a daughter—and not only because she's female, but because I think that I'll see myself in her, with all my anxieties and frailties.

Will she feel a freedom to engage in the world? Will she enjoy a boldness to be herself and accept herself as she is?

The following evening after the infant care class, Eric and I took a breastfeeding class at the medical center. Again, I gained more confidence, knowing almost all of the material, and feeling good about helping to teach Eric how he can take care of our daughter.

Eric is very excited to become a father, and he has been reading a book meant for new dads, which I'm really grateful for, because apparently the book helps him know how he can indirectly take care of the baby by taking care of me too. I'm not worried about the learning curve Eric will experience when we bring Baby home with us. He has consistently shown himself to be very adaptable. He isn't without insecurities, but I think that he knows he can expose all of them to me, the same way he wants me to feel about revealing all of me to him.

I can't wait to see Eric bond with our baby. When I squeal over the tiny clothes she has been gifted, Eric just smiles, seemingly more enamored with my glee than the thought of how adorable our newborn will be. Sometimes he playfully imitates me; he knows how to make me laugh.

At night, after our breastfeeding class, I was brushing my teeth in the bathroom and heard Eric talking to Lucky in the bedroom, in his playful voice where he imitates me. Toothbrush still in my mouth, looking into our room to see what was going on, I found Eric lying on our bed with his shirt off, with our Jack Russell Chihuahua on his belly, as he stroked her little back.

"Oxytocin," Eric explained, matter-of-fact. "Lucky and I are practicing skin-to-skin. Right, Lucky?"

I had to run to the sink before I spewed toothpaste everywhere, totally cracking up.

How did I get so lucky to be with this man?

Eric and I talked more about having a scheduled c-section. Even understanding I'll need to especially rely on him after a c-section, he has expressed full support of whichever birth method I choose. Through my discussions with Eric, I shifted in my perception of how I was making my decision.

Choosing a c-section isn't really a fear-based decision but an informed one. I know I have problems with panic and dissociation, and it is objectively reasonable to consider I may have those reactions to childbirth, with all its exposure and intrusion. Given those risks, I believe I'll enter motherhood much more easily and more confidently with a c-section delivery. I don't want my first hours and possibly days with my baby to be fraught with disorientation and dread. Just as I accept and respect my need to be vigilant with postpartum mood episodes, I accept my need to feel safe and give myself compassionate permission to make choices that are best for the me that I am right now.

I have been feeling great. Sometimes, by the end of the day, my back is a little achy, but that's okay. I've also noticed my energy level drops off at the end of the day too, but I know that's a combination of hormones and the common mild anemia I've developed as my blood volume has increased faster than my red blood cell production has. I'm still able to exercise, but I notice that I get winded easier when zooming up stairs.

If I weren't pregnant, this sort of fatigue would hint at depression, where, first I'm just fatigued, and then later as depression progresses, I'm chronically exhausted. It's hard to do anything in depression, making my bed especially desirable, goading the vicious cycle.

Getting out of bed was impossible for much of my hospitalization at Springview during D5. The loss of psychic energy was one thing, but my physical energy was so low too. My unit at Springview held a full schedule each day, which included a few group meetings, meals, and outdoor walks, but it also included an individual daily check-in with one of the staff, in addition to being seen by the psychiatrist Dr. Douglas, my nurse, and usually the social worker Jaime too. I don't remember most of D5 at Springview, but I'll never forget one of these staff check-ins, with a guy named Adam.

"Are you going to go to any groups today?" Adam asked, leaning back in his chair across from mine, outside on the deck on that warm summer Saturday morning.

I shrugged, looking to the ground. I hated being there. Making it through a day, just to wake up again and face yet another gruesome day, was so painful that I tried to pass as much time as possible in bed striving—never with any success—to just sleep.

"What are you going to do if you don't go to group this morning?" Adam asked.

Adam was probably a couple years older than me, tall and slim, who usually wore a plaid shirt. In Springview, I just wanted to be left alone; it was too much effort to talk to people. But I didn't mind if Adam was around—if he got a cup of coffee while I drank mine alone in the kitchen, or if he sat nearby while I waited to see my nurse. Adam reminded me for some reason of my older brother, with whom I was never that close to growing up but still had a deep fondness for. Adam didn't say much, and even when he said nothing at all, somehow I didn't feel so *alone* when Adam was nearby.

"Tell you what I think," Adam said, as I sat mutely examining my shoelaces. "I think you should try something different. You've been spending a lot of time in bed."

And I was ready to head right back there after that check-in.

Adam pulled out the paper that had our schedule for the day on it from his back pocket, unfolded it, and gave it a look-over.

"There's a lot you can do today. I think staying out of room today will help you feel better. Take your mind off things, get outside some. It's a nice day. What do you think?"

I shrugged. I didn't think anything could honestly help.

It was as if Adam read my mind.

"It might not help. But…on the other hand, it could," he said. "Do you think you could try it today? Attend everything on the schedule, and stay out of your bed the whole day?"

I looked to Adam. There was no hint of judgment in his face.

I'd be wasting my effort all day, I thought, but I agreed to the idea nonetheless.

"Okay," he said, with the subtlest grin. "Then I'm going to hold you accountable to it. You'll stay out of your room today. Fair?"

I nodded. "Fair," I said, and we stood up. I followed him to the back door, which he unlocked, and I entered the unit again. I grabbed a copy of the daily schedule and made my way to the first activity.

And I went to every one of them.

Sometime in the afternoon, the activity of the hour was a group walk outside. I went to my room to grab a bottle of Gatorade and my sunglasses. I'd just opened the small chest of drawers by my bed for my shades, when Adam's friendly voice called to me from right outside the hall.

"Katie, whatcha doing in your room?"

I had a small laugh. "Just grabbing my sunglasses. We're about to go outside."

I had *laughed*.

It's not to say that the day was easy. I'm sure I thought about suicide, and inexplicable tears probably came to my eyes behind those sunglasses on our walk. But I made it through the day, and at the end of it, I was utterly exhausted.

This accomplishment couldn't have been possible at the beginning of my hospitalization. I simply couldn't function. You might not understand what that's like, but it's the same inability to think and move in depression as my inability in hypomania to slow myself down and relax and will my mind to focus.

When I was back on the same unit only four months after D5, abounding with energy, the same staff member who had tried encouraging me to get out of bed in D5 had to tell me to stop running in the halls.

Bipolar disorder for me has such extreme poles of energy.

At the end of Week 35, I had my appointment with the lactation consultant, Dr. Jessica Hartley. It went quite differently than I'd expected.

For starters, I was already wary of seeing a lactation consultant, fearing I might get assigned to one who would be so focused on achieving exclusive breastfeeding that they wouldn't be able to help me accommodate my sleep needs. Obviously I've never had any of my own personal experience with lactation consultants, but I know many have dubbed them the "breast brigade" and have found their appointments with them and their unwelcomed visits in the hospital to be irritatingly pushy.

My clan of health professionals unfortunately often bears a similar rap. Dietitians can be inflexible and unrealistic, and while we decry the damaging diet-centric culture in which we live, dietitians are so often guilty of promulgating an unnatural relationship with food. It really bothers me when dietitians burden patients with food rules instead of teaching them basic nutrition science, which ultimately proves to incorporate a splendid variety of foods to not only support a healthy body but to enjoy *life* too. Maybe it's because of my own mental health problems that I am so concerned about nutrition counseling that focuses on quality of life. Anyway, I was a little bit prepared to put up my guard if a lactation consultant couldn't see the big picture.

But then my unease intensified. It happened right after the office called to confirm my appointment.

'Jessica Hartley,' I thought. 'Where have I heard that name?'

And then I made the connection: Dr. Hartley, an OB and lactation consultant, leads my hospital's "Baby-Friendly Hospital Initiative"—a program I feared focuses more on achieving specific outcomes on their own agenda while neglecting personal patient goals. I feared my concerns would be overlooked in order to breastfeed at all costs.

Flexibility with breastfeeding and access to nursery care are important needs for new moms with bipolar disorder. But I'm afraid that, given that the average age of bipolar disorder's onset is near the age of first pregnancies, many women are inadequately equipped with strategies to effectively communicate and advocate for their special needs.

I felt like cancelling the appointment. But I kept it, hoping to at least glean some bit of useful knowledge even if the doctor was focused on pushing an agenda.

Dr. Hartley had an easy-going manner, and after the initial pleasantries, she got down to business.

"What can I help you with today?" she asked.

'I bet I'm the only inept woman who she's ever seen with breastfeeding problems even *before* trying to breastfeed,' I thought, suddenly embarrassed.

I briefly explained my concerns about being able to breastfeed and also bottle feed, while obtaining a sufficient stretch of sleep each night.

"We can talk about ideas," she said, understandingly. And then she knocked my defenses right down. "What are *your* goals?"

The rest of the appointment was very humbling. Just as I'd assumed the high-risk OB I saw earlier in pregnancy would focus on my mental illness, I assumed Dr. Hartley would have a one-size-fits-all approach with me. Instead, just like Dr. Rebekah Stein had, she asked me what *my* priorities and concerns were first.

Not only were we able to discuss using a bottle right away when Baby is born, we were able to talk about formula. In fact, Dr. Hartley even thought some formula in my situation was better than exclusive breast milk.

"While each of your medications are deemed safe for breastfeeding individually," she explained, "the combination of them aren't ideal." Since I take these medications at night and their levels in my blood are highest at night, this would be the best time to use formula instead. This means that any of Eric's feeds overnight can simply use formula.

Dr. Hartley also said that many women with my rape history find breastfeeding to be triggering. She encouraged me that, if this happens with me, the baby will grow healthy and thrive just fine drinking formula.

I know this will be a trial-and-error process, and Dr. Hartley told me so also, but she made me feel really heartened about our plan. When I left, instead of feeling down on myself for not being able to exclusively breastfeed, I felt glad for likely being able to give her some—perhaps even *mostly*—breast milk.

It is now Week 36. Things are going so smoothly. My physical health and mental health are excellent. My side projects are humming along to my satisfaction. My marriage is easy-going, and I'm enjoying time with friends—now also seeing my favorite friend Cat more often, since she has picked up swimming for triathlons. I think Cat is a rock star athlete, and she always makes me feel like a badass for still being so active in my ninth month of pregnancy.

So now, Eric and I have things all in place. The nursery is all set, her diapers stocked up. The car seat is installed, and my hospital bag is ready.

But am *I* ready?

Chapter 10. Weeks 37-40

I married Eric on a beautiful Hawaiian evening in June, with a reception by the magical Pacific Ocean with our closest family and friends. With wine and tropical cocktails, Eric and I drank in the glorious sunset together, and as it sank below the perfect aqua waters, the music rose up and our friends began dancing. The trade winds breezed through the bottom of the light blush-colored skirt of my wedding gown, my sparkling shoes ditched under some table with everyone else's. A bridesmaid placed a haku lei—a beautiful floral wreath—on my head, my long straight blonde hair made up into an exquisite braided bun, leaving my slender, tan back bare above the lacy bodice of my gown. I held Eric's hand, rings symbolizing lifelong promises on our fingers—to have, to hold, to cherish, in sickness, and in health.

Exactly one year after this perfect night, Eric and I looked into each other's eyes. He held my hands, our rings still on our fingers. He gave me a soft kiss, and we said goodnight.

Without a word, the woman standing behind Eric gave us a gentle smile, and Eric turned to follow her. Using a key on her wrist, she unlocked the door, holding it open for Eric to pass through, and then quietly closed it behind him.

That night, our first anniversary night, I slept alone in a twin-sized bed with white bleached sheets, a weighted blanket draped over me where Eric's arm was supposed to be.

And I cried.

I spent my first wedding anniversary at Springview Hospital. Eric went home alone to an empty house, having to leave behind his suffering wife whose sickness he could not cure. Eric deserved better, and I wished he didn't have me in his life causing him pain, and I wished I could end my life and my own pain, too.

In sickness and in health. Eric is with me, and I am with Eric.

Here in Week 37, Eric and I celebrated our second anniversary. In stark contrast to last year, we had a wonderful night of intimate celebration—intimate in that we know and love and trust each other in greater depths and in new dimensions, having discovered and come to cherish new facets in one another with the life we share as husband and wife. With the joy of this intimacy, I can't imagine the magnificence of the journey our marriage will take.

We talked and we laughed over dinner. Everything was so easy.

I wish everything were always so easy. I wish I always were my Usual Self, like this.

We went all-out on the romance and, well, other things not possible in a locked unit where you have a roommate and are checked on every other minute. If you know what I mean.

Aw heck, I'll tell you a secret: Such things inpatient *are* actually possible, if one is clever enough, and one has a pass to leave the unit with one's spouse while still remaining on hospital grounds.

Dude don't tattle. A whole month in a psych hospital is a long time. And, if anything, planning such an escapade is a fantastic sign of improvement of depression, because to devise such a scheme evidences the beginnings of the reappearance of one's

Bipolar and Pregnant

Usual Self, such as occurred a couple weeks after my first wedding anniversary, soon before I returned home.

So. Changing the subject...

I had a classic "false alarm" of labor this week in Week 37. On Sunday before church, I convinced Eric to come on a short run with me. (The tables have turned now; it is Eric who has to keep his pace really slow to keep in step with his partner.)

"Hang on," I said to Eric as we were slowly making our way up a hill. I stopped and placed my hands on my belly. "Another contraction."

I waited stilly, until the hard, tight ball of my abdomen released itself about ten seconds later. I usually get one or two of these each workout—harmless Braxton-Hicks contractions that aren't a sign of impending labor. But this was my fourth one on this run.

"Babe?" Eric said. "You sure you're okay? Should we walk it home?"

"Nah, I'm totally fine. Nothing to worry about; these are normal." But another contraction kicked up only a couple minutes later. Eric didn't say anything, and neither did I, as I stopped on the sidewalk, again waiting for it to release.

We arrived home a couple minutes later, and I took a shower.

These were just Braxton-Hicks contractions, right? I wasn't going into labor, right?

I quickly dried off and put my bathrobe on, then placed my laptop on the counter and slid up to a bar stool. I looked up contractions and signs of labor, reassuring myself that I didn't have painful contractions or ones that lasted very long. I told Eric I was fine and, no, I didn't need to call the OB office.

But then I had another one.

I jumped up.

This was only Week 37. I still had over two weeks until my scheduled c-section—which I've fully expected to be Baby's delivery date. But what if she was going to come early? What if she was going to come *now*?

I paced. And then I paced with a dust cloth, some bathroom cleaner, a vacuum, picking up speed with each room I cleaned.

"Are you worried?" Eric asked me.

"No," I said, nodding my head yes.

"Would it help to talk to a nurse on the phone? Someone to confirm this is just Braxton-Hicks'?"

"Yeah," I said, shaking my head no.

I told him I believed my contractions really weren't labor, but that I was uneasy nonetheless. I told him I just needed to relax.

"*Can* you relax?" he asked.

I sighed. I explained I didn't want to make a phone call and look like an alarmist. It's a recurring concern of mine—to bother a professional for something trivial, or to be concerned about a symptom that really didn't signify anything.

In D2, after I swallowed a whole bottle of Tylenol and then became afraid, I balked at calling my psychiatrist, Dr. J.

'It's late,' I thought. 'This will be such a hassle for her. She has her own life.'

In the moment, I was more afraid of disrupting Dr. J's evening than of what would happen to my body if I didn't get medical attention.

Eric pointed out that pager numbers and on-call nurses and doctors were there for a reason, and he encouraged me to go ahead and call. The worst that could happen, he persuaded me, was they'd tell me it was a false alarm—which, he said, probably happened all day long in their line of work.

I called the number, left a message with the receptionist, and a couple minutes later, a nurse phoned me back. Just answering her questions reassured me. I wasn't in pain, I wasn't having any bleeding, and the contractions weren't getting stronger.

The nurse was very kind and told me to sit down and rest and to drink a whole liter of water. She asked me to call her back if they didn't subside in an hour.

"Okay," I said. "Thank you."

"Would you prefer for me to call you in an hour, to check up on you?" she offered.

I declined her offer. Not only did this nurse refrain from any condescension, she welcomed my need for assurance.

I put my feet up the next hour, drinking a few glasses of cucumber water brought to me by my supportive husband. Having no more contractions, I realized I had probably been quite dehydrated—a common instigator of Braxton-Hicks contractions. The day before—Saturday—I'd spent the hot summer afternoon at the pool with Eric, and I hadn't drunk much before Eric and I went on our jog that morning, too.

I felt reassured. But I also didn't feel embarrassed that I'd been concerned.

Holly would have been proud.

Without Eric, I'd probably have continued worrying in solitude. He is so supportive, and I look over this pregnancy and am amazed at how much he has helped me. He keeps me from plunging into pessimism, and he helps me see the blessings all around me. He doesn't judge me, and he is a haven of space for me to speak my mind and be myself.

Eric has been the role model of encouragement in our relationship, and, more recently, I've been given the opportunity to return the support. Eric is struggling with a career decision. He has three different opportunities that would each lead his career down different paths, and he hasn't made this difficult decision yet.

I appreciate that he's so carefully considering the three jobs. Each job is in a different state, with different pros and cons in regards to climate, cost of living, schools, proximity to family, job opportunities for me, and—something Eric has not overlooked—health care.

No matter where we move, I'm going to have to make brand-new relationships. New friends, new church members, and a new "Holly" and "Dr. C." I'll have to start over.

Will I be able to build support as a new mother? Will I be able to build support before another episode strikes again?

Bipolar and Pregnant

As you know, I'm a Planner who craves predictability. Normally it would feel so stressful having such a huge unknown hanging above me. But I'm not worried. Is this because I have such a big change—motherhood—right in front of me? Or is this maybe because I've developed some kernel of trust that Eric will look out for me, and that he'll hold my hand if the road ahead gets dark or bumpy?

As Eric wrestles with his career decision, I've thought about my own future career. I've been working as lead author on a meta-analysis of caffeine's effects on endurance athletic events with a couple statisticians, and I really enjoy sports nutrition. Should I pursue a private practice in this field? Should I get more experience in clinical dietetics? Should I write a nutrition book — maybe for athletes, or maybe for pregnant women?

There is so much yet before me. I have so much still to do with my life—my life with Eric, our lives with our daughter.

We finally hit Week 38. My pregnancy is now considered "full term", meaning that if Baby is born now, she won't be considered premature. She feels so big now, inside of me. Her movements are large enough to wake me up, and Lucky feels them too, when she snuggles close to me. The baby's hiccups are a favorite crowd pleaser; I welcome my friends' hands feeling her move, just thin layers of flesh separating us from her.

I have still been feeling very well, even this late in pregnancy. The summer heat hasn't bothered me anything out of the ordinary, and I don't feel fatigued. But, by the end of the day, my back does ache a little. Eric has been helping me by giving me some lower backrubs and handling the household chores like unloading the dishwasher that require a lot of bending. Swimming feels good for my back, and I have been doing some prenatal back exercises, but, ultimately, I suppose a thirty-plus pound weight gain was bound to cause some strain.

Aside from the backaches, I haven't minded the weight gain at all. In fact, I've quietly been proud of my body. Without much thoughtfulness about nutrition, save consuming a better variety of foods than usual, my body has basically managed to grow this baby on its own; I've been hungrier, so I've been eating more, and the weight effortlessly added up just like it was supposed to. With a GI disease with unpredictable exacerbations, an autoimmune thyroid disorder that has caused a dangerous tripling of metabolic hormones, and all the symptoms I've had with bipolar disorder, I have sometimes felt as though my own body is against me. So, to see the big baby bump grow right in front of me, and to see the gradual transformation these past nine months of my sharp bones and features to softer lines with a more inviting fullness gives me a gladness I hadn't anticipated.

Sometimes women with a trauma history like mine have a difficult time with the dramatic changes in pregnancy, because to some it can feel like their body is operating outside their control. That feeling of helplessness over your own body can be very triggering. I am thankful I have not struggled this way with the changes.

I keep my gladness with my pregnant body to myself, because I suspect most pregnant women don't welcome the weight gain that comes through supporting the healthy growth of a baby. Given that *most* American women are overweight and *most* American women report they are trying to lose weight, the routine weigh-ins at the OB office probably come with mixed emotions. I'm sure it's a lot easier for me to welcome my body's changes because I was underweight to begin with.

Though I have a tall and slim body that is often desired in our culture doesn't matter; proximity to any ideal hasn't made a difference in other areas of my life where I feel perpetually inadequate despite perfectionistic efforts. That my sense of

Bipolar and Pregnant

inadequacy hasn't touched my physical appearance is an example of the arbitrary nature of my irrational expectations. It is without even a glimmer of arrogance on my part that I can say I like my body, because I think that my acceptance of it must come in large part from something inside me not up to me, and this enables me to have compassion for other women who wish they had a different body.

What if I struggled with body image? Would the rapid changes in my size—not to mention all the feelings of bloating—make pregnancy a much more difficult journey?

And, with bipolar disorder, what if I was like *most* women and was trying to lose weight? Would the common side effect of weight gain in most of the drugs used to treat bipolar disorder be a strong deterrent to taking them?

Are OB's sensitive to body image issues and supporting healthy weight gain? Are psychiatrists equipped with counseling strategies to help bipolar patients weigh the costs and benefits of their medications that come with side effects? Do they have professional relationships with Registered Dietitians who can help mitigate drug-induced weight gain—experts who can help the patient refocus their goals on overall health—body, mind, and spirit—as a bipolar and pregnant woman?

July 4 came in Week 38. Eric and I grilled outside by the pool, and then we went to a nearby town to watch fireworks. I smiled at all the children in awe over the fireworks.

"Only ten more days," we kept saying to each other. Ten more days until Baby arrives, ten days till we become parents.

I think I'm ready. I want to say I'm ready. But I don't have to look very far in my rearview mirror to see that this day, just one year ago, I was in the hospital at Springview, unable to care for myself.

What do other parents worry about? What are the Normal Fears of parenthood?

I've read that prenatal maternal cortisol negatively impacts neurodevelopment of infants, but not in infants who develop secure attachment with their mothers. I'm doing my very best with anxiety right now, but it is very encouraging that there is so much more I can do for my baby when she arrives in my arms.

I can nurture good attachment. I know I can, because I strongly want to, and I have people in my life to help me. And I know I can help these people like Eric develop secure attachment with her too, to provide for her the safe and loving village it will take to raise her.

Right?

Week 39 came. I had my last appointment with Dr. Greenberg, now only four days away from Baby's delivery. As good luck would have it, she told me that Dr. Jessica Hartley—that lactation specialist—would be the OB delivering my baby.

I can't believe I've nearly made it through the whole pregnancy. From the gripping fears I had about being pregnant my first appointment with Dr. Greenberg, to now the excited anticipation I have in counting down the days till Baby's arrival, I've come such a long way.

I love writing—novels, screenplays, and, most of all, poetry. I've tried to express myself in this journal, to imprint who I am, in single tableaus, and also through stories and backstories, to show you the overall person of Katie McDowell. I enjoy these attempts to infuse my life into words through memoir. But poetry is my favorite art.

There is a high prevalence of mental illness in artists, at the staggering rate of about ten times the general population's prevalence, I've read. Depression and bipolar disorder have run rampant in the greatest poets—sadly, with approximately one in five committing suicide. Maybe we need to feel things deeply to transform emotions into words. Maybe it takes experiencing the extremes to appreciate the ever-changing, mutable nature of life. And how this is beautiful.

I look back on my journal, and I can't miss seeing the character arc of myself over these past nine months. This hasn't been a steady journey. I'm not a static person. I'll rise, and I'll fall; I'll go through setbacks and achievements.

I'm going to have some significant highs, and I'm going to have some drastic lows. This is bipolar disorder.

And this is Life.

What will the arc of my person look like across my life? I've read that, in people with Bipolar II like me, subclinical depression becomes more prevalent with subsequent mood episodes. Maybe there is a neurochemical basis for this, or maybe going through life with the illness is simply disheartening. My mood episodes have been pretty distinct, and I believe that my mental health during periods of my Usual Self—which is *most* of the time, is good. Will it always be like this?

Can I promote healthy maintenance? Can I keep growing? Can I give and receive love and support, build up my marriage and friendships, and develop a closer relationship with God—the things that make life—even life with mental illness—worth living?

After seeing Dr. Greenberg, I went to my last appointment with Holly before the baby comes. I had some spare time and a hankering for ice cream, so I decided to stop for some at a place I'd been before, in between their offices, which was in Springview's neighborhood.

I didn't want to go there. But I knew I needed to.

I parked my car and walked down the sidewalk, welcoming the cool air as I stepped inside. I looked through the glass at the delicious variety of flavors, deciding on a scoop of cookies and cream and one of chai.

My dad used to take us to get ice cream, when we were little. He usually didn't tell us we were going there; it was on the way home, and he would just delight us by making the stop. I loved looking at all the different flavors behind the glass. To a little kid, there seemed to be a hundred. But I always got rocky road. Because Dad did.

Ice cream is going to be Our thing, I decided. Me and my daughter.

I took my treat out to a bench on the sidewalk, basking in the warm, summer day, my sundress accentuating the bundle in my belly. I savored the ice cream, the sunshine, the people strolling along the sidewalks.

Down the street, across some train tracks, and up a hill, was Springview Hospital. Where I was diagnosed with bipolar disorder, and where the baby, who will enter the world in just four days, was already beginning to grow, without my even knowing of her.

Bipolar and Pregnant

People entered the ice cream shop behind me. A couple passed in front of me, smiling my way at my baby bump. Across the street, a few kids bubbled out of a coffee shop, followed by a mom, hands full with cold beverages. Cars drove by, heading in each direction, people going Somewhere, to do Something.

So many people. People with desires, with goals, with plans.

People with issues, with obstacles, with troubles.

To anyone walking by, I'm just a young woman, ripe with pregnancy, getting even tanner in her cotton dress and colorful sandals, seemingly carefree. They don't know I have bipolar disorder.

They don't know we're all so much alike.

I finished my ice cream, walked back to my car, and drove onward to Holly's—the old yellow house of therapy suites on the corner, the trees full and green, the flowers blooming all along the way. I'd tell her about my excitement for Friday—when I'll meet Baby, about the preparations for the hospital stay, and about my plans for going home, with Eric taking care of me, in our new family of three.

And I'd tell her of my bravery, in stopping by Springview. Of what I was honoring: the one-year anniversary of my D5 discharge there.

My acceptance, my sweet self-compassion.

The big day finally came. Eric and I were excited beyond words on the drive to the hospital. I was a little nervous the day before, but then Eric and I went out to enjoy something very rich and loaded with butter for dinner, followed by something very rich and loaded with sugar for dessert, before coming home to have sex in the shower (hopefully by now you've gotten over it, prudes). I couldn't wait to meet her.

We arrived at the labor and delivery floor, for my 8am check-in time. A nurse took us to my room, and I changed into a gown. Various doctors came in to see me, explaining their roles.

I was brought into the operating room, where several nurses and doctors were prepping. The anesthesiologist had me sit on the edge of the operation table and instructed me to remain very still, because he was going to inject the spinal block into my back, which would numb me from my chest down. Another doctor stood in front of me and asked me to lean forward onto her shoulder to help me remain still. As she put her arm around my back, it felt like a hug, and I relaxed.

Once I was draped and the surgeons were almost ready to begin, they brought Eric in. He sat down right beside me, on our side of the drape that separated my chest from my abdomen, and he held my hand.

The incisions were very quick, and I felt no pain.

"We're going to deliver your baby now," the anesthesiologist said. They pulled down the blue drape separating me from the surgeons, with a clear drape remaining up, so that I could see.

Eric held my hand.

My husband, my Partner in Life, my best friend.

I felt some gentle tugging, then the most beautiful sound I'd ever heard filled the room—our daughter crying. Our baby.

After quickly being examined by a doctor, Eric went over to cut her umbilical cord. Separated from me, but a part of me.

Bipolar and Pregnant

Eric brought our baby over to me and they tenderly laid her on my chest. I felt her soft skin, on mine, her heartbeat, my heartbeat.

And I cried. With joy.

***

These past 40 weeks have been an incredible journey for me—through bipolar disorder and pregnancy. Thank you for taking it with me.

It was a joy to experience the most special time of womanhood I ever have, and I'm very grateful for it. No longer pregnant, this chapter has closed for now.

But I will always have bipolar disorder. I hope that my mood episodes will be few and far between, and that they won't ever reach the severity they have in my past. But I acknowledge that times of wellness won't mean bipolar has left me but that it is simply in remission. Bipolar disorder is part of who I am.

But it is not all of me. I am a wife, a daughter, a sister, and a friend. I am a Christian. I am a writer, a poet, and a lover of good books.

And I remain an outgoing introvert, a disciplined lover of routine, someone who is not spontaneous or adventurous but craves predictability. I am prone to worry, I plan ahead, and I still love the comfort of a good comfort zone. I am forgiving, and I am resilient. I am always learning, and I am always growing.

And now, I am a mother.

Made in the USA
Monee, IL
31 January 2025